100

THINGS TO DO IN
AMERICA
BEFORE YOU
DIE

100

THINGS TO DO IN
AMERICA
BEFORE YOU
DIE

● ● ● ● ● ● ● ● ● ● ● ● ●

BILL CLEVLEN

Library of Congress Control Number: 2017934670

ISBN: 9781681061016

Design by Jill Halpin

Cover Image: A patriotic fence in LeClaire, IA (Photo: Bill Clevlen)

Printed in the United States of America
17 18 19 20 21   5 4 3 2 1

Please note that websites, phone numbers, addresses, and company names are subject to change or cancellation. We did our best to relay the most accurate information available, but due to circumstances beyond our control, please do not hold us liable for misinformation. When exploring new destinations, please do your homework before you go.

DEDICATION

This book is dedicated to the thousands of kind Americans I have met during my travels across the country. Thank you all for constantly reminding me that the United States remains a place full of hopeful, decent, and patriotic people.

• •

CONTENTS

Amusements and Entertainment

• •

• •

Sports and Recreation

• •

Photo Ops

Road Trips

• •

American History and Culture

• •

● ●

OHIO
HISTORICAL MARKER

BIRTHPLACE OF ROCK 'N' ROLL

When radio station WJW disc jockey Alan Freed (1921-1965) us
the term "rock and roll" to describe the uptempo black rhy
and blues records he played beginning in 1951, he named a
genre of popular music that appealed to audiences on both
of 1950s American racial boundaries — and dominated Am
culture for the rest of the 20th century. The popul
Freed's nightly "Moon Dog House Rock and Roll Par
show encouraged him to organize the Moondog Corone
the first rock concert. Held at the Cleveland Arena
1952, the oversold show was beset by a riot
first set. Freed, a charter inductee into the Rock
of Fame, moved to WINS in New York City in 195
to promote rock music through radio, tele
and live performances.

THE OHIO BICENTENNIAL COMMI
THE ROCK AND ROLL HALL OF
THE OHIO HISTORICAL SOC
2003

PREFACE

In the spring of 2013, I launched a travel website and radio program called "Bill on the Road." Little did I know how much the risk of starting a new career with almost zero experience in the travel or tourism industry would wind up paying off. I've visited hundreds of cities, made countless new friends in every corner of the country, and met the love of my life—all thanks to taking road trips across America.

Someone asked me early on why I chose to focus on the United States when so many travel writers spend most of their time exploring other countries. For me, the answer was pretty simple. As Americans, we are so blessed and fortunate that we often forget what an incredible place we have to call home, whether it's the charming small towns in every state; the beauty of beachfronts, lakes, and mountains; or the rich history that's waiting to be discovered around every corner of every road.

When compiling any kind of list, especially in a book, you always run the risk of leaving something out or adding something people will disagree with. *100 Things to Do in America Before You Die* isn't a definitive list. It's just a place to start.

My goal was to write a book that could potentially serve as a guide for someone who knows nothing about the United States of America. After careful thought and debate and a living room floor full of index cards, I came up with my best 100 suggestions that should make anyone completely understand what America is all about. These are sights, sounds, tastes, and experiences that tell the American story through travel.

• •

My hope is that these suggestions will inspire family vacations or solo road trips, or simply serve as a gentle reminder of why we're so fortunate to be Americans.

Remember every road leads to another great destination. Get out there and rediscover America for yourself.

Bill Clevlen

ACKNOWLEDGMENTS

In the summer of 2016, Josh Stevens of Reedy Press contacted me about writing a book after learning about my travel website, billontheroad.com. Josh, Barbara, and the entire team at Reedy Press have been beyond incredible to work with. (And no, they didn't slip this into the book after editing.)

I want to thank my dad, who never turns down the chance to join me on a road trip and taught me to be positive. Dolsee, thank you for listening to me talk about this book almost every day for nearly six months. You're the most supportive and caring person I've ever met, and I love you to the moon and back.

Pat Davenport, thanks for buying me a new chair so I didn't have to write this book on the floor.

Thanks to other travel writers who have been so gracious. It's a tough and often cutthroat business. Instead of competition, I've found wisdom, support, and encouragement whenever I've asked for it.

Finally, I want to thank all of you who regularly read or listen to my stories. You'll no doubt be the first ones to buy this book, and I can't thank you enough. Your support has allowed me to experience so many things that once seemed impossible.

AMUSEMENTS AND ENTERTAINMENT

CELEBRATE NEW YEAR'S EVE
IN TIMES SQUARE

An estimated one million people gather in Times Square to watch the ball drop on New Year's Eve in New York City. Another 100 million Americans will watch the countdown unfold on television or online, making it perhaps the single most watched event in the United States.

The best piece of advice for taking part in the celebration? Get there early. It's free to attend, but be prepared to spend big bucks if you want to stay at a hotel or even grab a bite to eat at a nearby restaurant. In 2015 even entry into a NYC Olive Garden cost a whopping $400 (admission, though, did include unlimited breadsticks).

Other impressive stats: A grand total of 32,256 LED lights are attached to the ball. More than 6,000 police officers are on duty during the event, and 3,000 pounds of confetti fall on attendees. Only twice has the ball not dropped: 1942 and 1943 during World War II.

timessquarenyc.org

ROAD TRIP TRIVIA QUESTION #1
Why did the tradition of dropping a ball in Times Square begin in the first place?

WATCH THE FIREWORKS
AT WALT DISNEY WORLD

Americans spend more than a billion dollars each year on fireworks. Whether we're shooting them off in our driveways or watching professional displays, there's no doubt that our country's desire for loud, colorful explosions isn't going away any time soon.

While many great backdrops can be found across the US for a fireworks display, nobody does it better than Walt Disney World in Orlando, Florida. Thousands of guests at the Magic Kingdom end their day of family fun by picking out a sweet spot on Main Street to soak in the incredible twelve-minute display. At an estimated cost of more than $30,000 a pop, the nightly presentation makes Disney the largest consumer of fireworks on the planet.

Guests enjoy 683 pieces of pyrotechnics with more than 500 different firing cues as the bright, colorful bursts of Disney magic erupt over Cinderella's castle.

Be sure to look for Tinkerbell as she magically flies from the castle and over the crowd, a tradition that's been in place since 1985.

ROAD TRIP TRIVIA QUESTION #2
What year did the first Disney fireworks show take place
at Disneyland in Southern California?

EXPERIENCE THE DRIVE-IN

In 1933 a man named Richard Hollingshead brought two great pieces of American culture together. It was in Camden, New Jersey, that the automobile and Hollywood were first perfectly combined with the invention of the drive-in theater.

There's something special about seeing a movie under the stars. It's typically more affordable than a high-tech multiplex, but don't fret about sacrificing picture quality or sound. In 2013 movie studios began converting to digital distribution, which meant existing drive-in locations had to convert or shut down. Besides better HD quality, audio is now played through your own vehicle's sound system.

Although the numbers are drastically down from the 1958 peak of more than 4,000 locations, you can still find drive-in movie theaters across the US, though they're mostly in rural parts of the country.

As of 2016, 324 were still open for business. Ohio boasts the most active drive-ins, while every other state still has at least one.

United Drive-in Theatre Owners Association
uditoa.org

ROAD TRIP TRIVIA QUESTION #3
Known for being a popular makeout spot for young lovers, what were drive-in theaters often called?

VISIT THE AMERICAN SIGN MUSEUM

When was the last time you stopped and really paid attention to the countless number of signs up and down the roads of your town? The American Sign Museum in Cincinnati brings deserved attention to the importance of signs in our nation's history and highlights the craftsmanship and creativity of the people who build and design them.

As you step inside, you're faced with a visual overload of aesthetically pleasing signage from every generation. You simply cannot look away. It's as though the mixture of signs from hotels, soda shops, gas stations, and beyond just sucks you in.

The collection includes more than six hundred pieces, ranging from small storefront signs to massive neon displays from McDonald's and Howard Johnson that seem to fill the entire room with bright, vibrant color. Strolling through the exhibits is a walk down memory lane and a brilliant reminder of how signs are so important in the commerce and culture of America. The museum also includes a working neon shop.

1330 Monmouth Ave.
Cincinnati, OH 45225
americansignmuseum.org

ROAD TRIP TRIVIA QUESTION #4

The famous McDonald's signs with the golden arches proudly display "Over 99 Billion Served," referring to the number of hamburgers sold. The fast-food chain sold its one billionth hamburger on live television in what year?

RIDE A CABLE CAR
IN SAN FRANCISCO

San Francisco's iconic cable car system was born as an alternative mode of transportation to eliminate injuries to horses pulling streetcars up the city's steep hills.

Each year ten million people take a ride on one of the forty cable cars currently in service. Traveling at speeds of 9.5 miles per hour, each car can carry more than sixty passengers at a time along one of the three dedicated cable car routes. The cars run seven days a week with special schedules on the weekends.

Cable cars are pulled by an underground cable equipped with a gripping mechanism that operates by a lever in the front. The entire underground operating system was refurbished in the early 1980s.

The San Francisco cable cars have the distinct honor of being the only National Historic Landmark that moves. Each summer a competition is held to determine the city's "Best Cable Car Bell Ringer."

sfcablecar.com

ROAD TRIP TRIVIA QUESTION #5
What 1993 Robin Williams movie featured a quick scene with a cable car operator?

IN THE NEIGHBORHOOD

Golden Gate Bridge
The most photographed bridge in the world is
1.7 miles long, connecting San Francisco and Marin
counties in California. Its unique color is called
"international orange," and its towers are 746 feet tall.
(A toll is charged to drive across.)

Golden Gate Bridge Welcome Center
415-426-5220
goldengate.org

Alcatraz Island
This former federal penitentiary closed in 1963 but is
currently open for tours, accessible by ferry from Pier 33.
It was thought to be "escape proof," as it's surrounded
by the cold waters and strong currents of San Francisco
Bay. Alcatraz housed 1,576 of America's most dangerous
criminals, the most notable being Al Capone.

415-561-4900
nps.gov/alca

Coit Tower
A 210-foot art deco tower offering a great 360° view of
San Francisco. An elevator takes guests to the observation
deck for a small fee. Located on historic Telegraph Hill, the
tower's base features popular murals from the 1930s.

1 Telegraph Hill Blvd.
San Francisco, CA 94133
415-249-0995
sfrecpark.org

WATCH A CATTLE DRIVE
AT THE FORT WORTH STOCKYARDS

The Fort Worth Stockyards was once the world's biggest market for horses and mules. Its nickname became "Wall Street of the West" due to the massive amount of business taking place. Between 1866 and 1890, drovers trailed more than four million head of cattle through Fort Worth thanks in large part to the railroad, which made the city a major shipping point.

The world's only twice-daily cattle drive takes place at 11:30 a.m. and 4 p.m., where spectators can watch the action in the stockyards (except on Easter, Thanksgiving, and Christmas).

The first indoor rodeo took place in the stockyards' Cowtown Coliseum. To this day, the venue still hosts rodeos and other forms of entertainment. In keeping with tradition, thousands of head of cattle are still sold from the Exchange Building, only now they are sold by satellite video.

Stockyards Visitor Center
130 East Exchange Ave.
Fort Worth, TX 76164
817-624-4741
fortworthstockyards.org

ROAD TRIP TRIVIA QUESTION #6
During the rodeo at the Fort Worth Stockyards, the crowd traditionally claps their hands in unison as what song is being played?

GO BACK IN TIME
AT WICHITA'S OLD COWTOWN MUSEUM

The Old Cowtown Museum in Wichita, Kansas, is a firsthand look at American life in the second half of the nineteenth century. Unlike a typical museum, Cowtown is a living time capsule of historic structures on an old dirt road along the banks of the Arkansas River. You can walk into each of the buildings and find costumed interpreters who will share stories and answer questions.

In addition to the fifty-four buildings, a 10,000-piece collection of furniture, tools, and documents helps tell the story of what life was like between 1865 and 1880.

While you stroll the grounds, you can enter the local jail, look at medicine in the drugstore, or have a seat in the town's church. One popular stop is Fritz Snitzler's Saloon, where you can order a sarsaparilla or perhaps witness a gunfight between two rowdy locals.

1865 W. Museum Blvd.
Wichita, KS 67203
316-219-1871
oldcowtown.org

ROAD TRIP TRIVIA QUESTION #7
Can you name the pizza restaurant chain that was founded in Wichita?

TAKE A TOUR
OF THE WINCHESTER MYSTERY HOUSE

Everyone deals with grief in different ways. Sarah Winchester dealt with the deaths of her child and husband by building what many claim is the most bizarre home in all of America. An heir to the Winchester rifle fortune, Sarah believed her family was being haunted by spirits of people killed by those guns. A Boston medium allegedly told Mrs. Winchester to move out west and build a home to house the spirits or she would be the next one to die.

The Victorian-style mansion in San Jose, California, was built without blueprints, and construction continued for nearly thirty-eight years around the clock. The house features staircases that lead nowhere and secret doors and chimneys that never reach the roof. Many believe the home is indeed haunted.

Guests can tour the miles of twisting hallways and secret passages along with a visit to the estate's immaculate garden. The mansion has 160 rooms, 40 bedrooms, 2 ballrooms, 17 chimneys, and more than 10,000 window panes.

525 S. Winchester Blvd.
San Jose, CA 95128
408-247-2000
winchestermysteryhouse.com

ROAD TRIP TRIVIA QUESTION #8
What once caused Mrs. Winchester to be trapped in her bedroom while a seven-story observation tower at the mansion toppled over?

DRINK FREE WATER AT WALL DRUG

While traveling along Highway 90 in South Dakota, you'll see sign after sign promoting Wall Drug, one of the state's most visited attractions. Open since 1931, the sprawling complex features shopping, dining, and, of course, free ice water for more than two million visitors each year.

In the early days of Wall Drug, business was bad. To help generate foot traffic, Ted and Dorothy Hustead created signs that offered free ice water to motorists passing through the area. The clever idea worked and put their small-town drugstore on the map.

Many of the highway billboards mention the number of miles you are from Wall Drug. Signs are also spread out around neighboring states and even in places around the world indicating the exact distance.

In his 1989 book *The Lost Continent*, Bill Bryson writes: "It's an awful place, one of the world's worst tourist traps, but I loved it, and I won't have a word said against it."

510 Main St.
Wall, SD 57790
605-279-2175
walldrug.com

ROAD TRIP TRIVIA QUESTION #9
You already know that ice water is free at Wall Drug,
but how much does a cup of coffee cost?

TRY NOT TO GET LOST
INSIDE THE BILTMORE ESTATE

Off the top of your head, how many wealthy people can you name? Now imagine what would happen if all the people you just thought of pooled their money together and built a house. That's pretty much what the Biltmore amounts to in Asheville, North Carolina.

The largest privately owned residence in America is surrounded by 8,000 acres of gardens and woodlands. The home itself is a staggering 178,926 square feet, which includes 250 rooms, 43 bathrooms, and 65 fireplaces. Built by George Washington Vanderbilt II in 1889, the estate took six years to complete and is truly beyond belief.

The high ceilings, bowling alley, library, and even the indoor pool will all take your breath away. (Some say the indoor pool is actually haunted.) The home has hosted US presidents and even stored priceless works of art during World War II.

Located on the property, the Biltmore Winery is currently the most visited winery in America, with more than 600,000 guests a year. More than 250 weddings are held on the grounds as well.

One Lodge St.
Asheville, NC 28803
800-411-3812
biltmore.com

ROAD TRIP TRIVIA QUESTION #10
One US president visited the Biltmore Estate and became so fascinated with a globe in the library that he put on gloves so that he could touch it and spin it around. Who was it?

SEE BIG THINGS
IN CASEY, ILLINOIS

The best part of an All-American road trip is pulling off the highway to see what I commonly refer to as "road quirk." The largest ball of twine, the world's biggest fork, or the tallest easel would all qualify as fun, uniquely American tourist stops.

The tiny town of Casey, Illinois, may have set the record for the most roadside attractions in the entire country. While not all the attractions are technically record setting, many of them are, with more on the way in the future.

A local man named Jim Bolin has a fascination with designing and building big things. His first piece was the world's largest wind chime. Other record setters include the world's tallest rocking chair, pitchfork, wooden shoes, knitting needles, crochet hook, and my favorite—the world's largest mailbox.

Casey is also home to the world's largest golf tee, which can be found at the city's local country club. It is thirty feet tall and weighs 6,659 pounds.

bigthingssmalltown.com

ROAD TRIP TRIVIA QUESTION #11
Weighing 46,200 pounds, the world's largest rocking chair had to literally rock to qualify for the world record. How many people did it take to make the chair rock?

STAY THE NIGHT
IN BUFFALO'S OCCIDENTAL HOTEL

Walking through the front door of the Occidental Hotel in Buffalo, Wyoming, is like stepping straight back into the Wild West. Whether you plan to stay overnight or just pop in for a look around, you'll appreciate the original ceilings still intact and the awesome back bar in the adjoining saloon, delivered by wagon more than a hundred years ago.

The Occidental welcomed many famous names of the Old West, such as Butch Cassidy and the Sundance Kid, Buffalo Bill Cody, and Tom Horn. Ernest Hemingway stayed here, as well as presidents Theodore Roosevelt and Herbert Hoover. The hotel also hosts celebrities who often go unnoticed. Singer John Mayer and actor Paul Giamatti are among some of the more recent notable guests.

The hotel is known for hosting popular bluegrass jam sessions with David Stewart, the current owner. He is a longtime songwriter and even once walked all the way to Nashville for a chance to play at the Grand Ole Opry.

10 N. Main St.
Buffalo, WY 82834
307-684-0451
occidentalwyoming.com

ROAD TRIP TRIVIA QUESTION #12
Wyoming has only one area code for all phone numbers in the entire state. What are the other states that also have just one area code?

GROUNDHOG DAY
IN PUNXSUTAWNEY

Since 1886, February 2 has been known to Americans as Groundhog Day. Phil (the groundhog) comes out of his burrow on Gobbler's Knob in front of a huge crowd to predict the weather for the rest of the winter. Legend has it that if the groundhog sees his shadow there will be six more weeks of cold weather. If he doesn't see his shadow there will be an early spring.

Visitors can see Punxsutawney Phil year-round at his burrow in Barclay Square, which is attached to the Punxsutawney Memorial Library.

The Punxsutawney Groundhog Club hosts various events leading up to the big day, including the annual Groundhog Ball. Of course the big event is a trek to see if Phil sees his shadow. It's suggested that you dress warmly and be prepared to stand if you decide to visit, as no chairs are available, and the festivities begin in the middle of the night.

301 E. Mahoning St., Suite 4
Punxsutawney, PA 15767
groundhog.org

ROAD TRIP TRIVIA QUESTION #13
What was the song that played every morning on the radio in the 1993 Bill Murray film *Groundhog Day*?

TOUR A GHOST TOWN

All across America you'll find communities that were completely abandoned. Some of these places eerily have everything still intact right down to cars in garages and food in the cupboards. A few have since been turned into tourist traps, but others still remain untouched and give you an authentic ghost town experience. The term "ghost town" is a bit misleading, though, as folks didn't leave because their homes were haunted; they left in most cases because there wasn't any work.

Most of these locations are former mining towns. The former residents once looked for such things as gold, copper, or coal. Some, for example, Batsto Village in New Jersey, were company towns that once produced materials. Smaller places, such as Cahawba, Alabama, closed after endless flooding.

Whatever the reason for being deserted, these towns are fascinating to visit and provide a living history lesson about early American life. They're also incredibly creepy.

ghosttowns.com

ROAD TRIP TRIVIA QUESTION #14
What state has the most ghost towns?

GHOST TOWN SUGGESTIONS

Dudleytown, CT

Often called the "village of the damned," it was abandoned in the late 1800s. Rumor is that if you take something from the town you'll be haunted by spirits.

Bodie, CA

A former gold-mining town that is now run by the state of California and is a National Historic Landmark.

Thurmond, WV

A former bustling coal town that's not completely abandoned. The 2010 Census showed the town is still occupied by five residents.

Terlingua, TX

Explore the ruins of the Chisos Mining Company and other abandoned buildings. The town still hosts a popular chili cookoff each November.

Kennecott, AK

Once a hot spot for copper mining, the town was empty by 1938. Guided tours are available to explore the buildings, including the town's iconic red mill.

SEE THE VACUUM CLEANER MUSEUM

This fun collection of more than six hundred working vacuum cleaners provides a great (free) way to see the progression of the typical American household. You begin by walking through a display of antique models from the 1900s, e.g., the Royal Model 1, and work your way through the decades of styles, colors, and sizes.

The collection mostly belongs to vacuum cleaner enthusiast and curator Tom Gasko. A chunk of his collection came from legendary organist (and fellow vacuum enthusiast) Stan Kann, who became famous as a frequent guest on *The Tonight Show Starring Johnny Carson,* where he'd bring out pieces of his vacuum collection.

The museum is located along historic Route 66 in Saint James, Missouri, in the back of the Tacony Manufacturing Plant, where Simplicity and Riccar vacuum cleaners are made. You can also ask for a free tour of the plant.

3 Industrial Dr.
St. James, MO 65559
866-444-9004
vacuummuseum.com

ROAD TRIP TRIVIA QUESTION #15
How did most early models of electric vacuums get power
before homes had wall outlets?

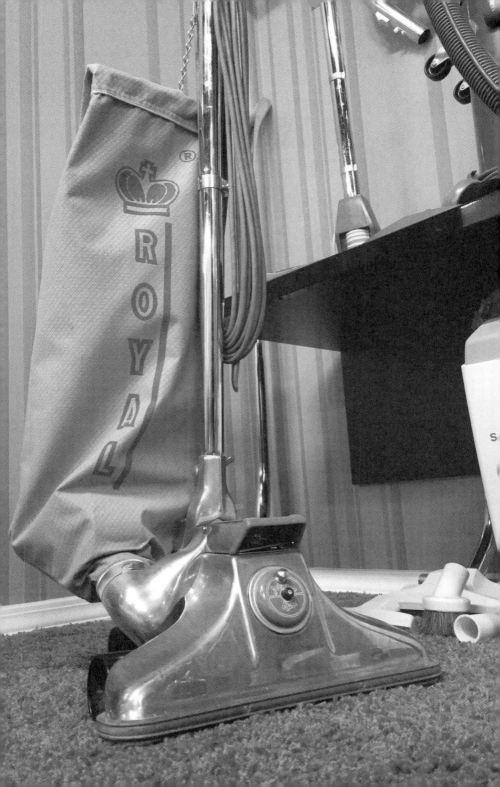

GO TO THE TOP
OF THE GATEWAY ARCH

Towering 630 feet above the city of Saint Louis on the banks of the Mississippi River, the Gateway Arch is a symbol of America's westward expansion. It is also the tallest man-made monument in the Western hemisphere.

Visitors can climb inside one of the eight trams located in both of the Arch legs. The experience has been described by some as climbing into a washing machine. Once you're inside, the retro capsule takes you on a four-minute ride all the way to the top. On the observation deck, you can see terrific views of downtown Saint Louis and into western Illinois on the other side of the river.

The Arch is built to withstand earthquakes and can sway as much as eighteen inches. More than five hundred tons of pressure was used to pry the north and south legs of the Arch apart for the final four-foot piece at the top. The windows are so small because larger ones wouldn't be able to withstand that pressure.

100 Washington Ave.
Saint Louis, MO 63102
877-982-1410
gatewayarch.com

ROAD TRIP TRIVIA QUESTION #16
How many windows are located at the top of the Gateway Arch?

IN THE NEIGHBORHOOD

Missouri History Museum

5700 Lindell Blvd.
Saint Louis, MO 63112
314-746-4599
mohistory.org

Busch Stadium & Cardinals Hall Of Fame

700 Clark Ave.
Saint Louis, MO 63102
314-345-9600
stlcardinals.com

Old Courthouse

11 N. Fourth St.
St. Louis, MO 63102
314-655-1600

Anheuser Busch Brewery

1200 Lynch St.
Saint Louis, MO 63118
314-577-2626
budweisertours.com

City Museum

750 N. Sixteenth St.
Saint Louis, MO 63103
314-231-2489
citymuseum.org

SEE A SHOW
AT A FOX THEATRE

In 1929 film pioneer William Fox built five majestic theaters to showcase his company's films in grand style. The remaining theaters are located in Saint Louis, Atlanta, and Detroit, while the other two in Brooklyn and San Francisco are no longer. When the Fox Theatre in Atlanta first opened its doors, a local newspaper columnist penned "the new Fox Theatre is picturesque and almost disturbing grandeur beyond imagination."

Each theater holds about 5,000 seats, but instead of showing films like their original purpose the venues now host concerts and touring musicals, such as *Mamma Mia!, Wicked,* or *Jersey Boys.* For fifty cents, patrons could enjoy music from organs, Fox Movietone News, and a film. The location in Saint Louis still has the original projector once used to show films.

527 N. Grand Blvd.
Saint Louis, MO 63103
fabulousfox.com

2211 Woodward Ave.
Detroit, MI 48201
olympiaentertainment.com

660 Peachtree St. NE
Atlanta, GA 30308
foxtheatre.org

ROAD TRIP TRIVIA QUESTION #17
Which of the Fox Theatre locations hosted
a presidential debate in 2016?

ATTEND SPACE CAMP

If you thought Space Camp was just for children, think again. Adults can sign up for Space Camp as well, and what an awesome experience awaits you. You'll use a replica mission control console, punch buttons, and give commands. You'll observe overhead monitors of other campers inside a replica space module completing vital tasks, all while in official astronaut gear. During your time at camp, you'll train in NASA simulators, such as the one that teaches you how to walk across the moon's surface.

The U.S. Space & Rocket Center in Huntsville, Alabama, houses awesome artifacts, including a Saturn 5 Moon Rocket that stretches 363 feet across a museum gallery. Other NASA history on display includes the Apollo 16 Command Module, an Apollo 12 moon rock, and a vehicle that transported astronauts, including Neil Armstrong, after they had returned to Earth. (The vehicle was used in case they had been "contaminated" while in space.)

1 Tranquility Base
Huntsville, AL 35805
800-637-7223
rocketcenter.com
spacecamp.com

ROAD TRIP TRIVIA QUESTION #18

Who is the only US president to have been on-site
during a shuttle launch?

SHOP AT PIKE PLACE MARKET
IN SEATTLE

Since 1907, Pike Place Market has been one of the country's most recognized shopping destinations. An icon of Seattle, the nine-acre venue features 85 local farmers, 225 artists, and 240 small ("mom and pop") businesses. Seventy of the businesses are restaurants or take-out stalls. About four hundred apartments house residents on the property, as well.

When visiting Pike Place Market, you can shop for fresh produce, buy a painting, or even get a tattoo or haircut. The market has a senior center, medical clinic, child care center, and food bank. Rachel the Piggy Bank is the market's mascot and a popular fund-raising tool. For good luck, you're supposed to rub the snout of the 750-pound bronze cast pig.

While shopping, you'll hear languages from all over the world, including Chinese, Hindi, Russian, Turkish, Japanese, French, and Arabic. Virginia Inn, the restaurant at First Avenue and Virginia Street, is the market's oldest business. It opened its doors in 1903—four years before the market opened.

1531 Western Ave.
Seattle, WA 98101
pikeplacemarket.org

ROAD TRIP TRIVIA QUESTION #19

As of 2017, half of Seattle's Fortune 500 companies ranked in the list's top 30 largest companies in America. Can you name all four of them?

STAY AT THE HOTEL HERSHEY

During the Depression, Milton Hershey faced the prospect of an entire town on welfare. Instead, he kept as many as eight hundred construction workers employed by building the beautiful Hotel Hershey. The 276-room, four-star hotel sits on a hill that overlooks "the sweetest place on Earth." It's also a member of the Historic Hotels of America.

The hotel may never have been built had history taken a different turn. Hershey had a ticket to board the Titanic in 1912 but didn't wind up using it.

By all accounts, Hershey was a great and generous man. As the founder of the Hershey Company, he left a lasting legacy on the town of Hershey, Pennsylvania, in many different ways. He transferred the bulk of his wealth to a trust fund that pays for a private grade school for children of low-income families. The Milton Hershey School, even a hundred years after its founding, still offers completely free tuition. Students also get free housing, health care, and meals.

100 Hotel Rd.
Hershey, PA 17033
717-533-2171
thehotelhershey.com

ROAD TRIP TRIVIA QUESTION #20

What was the last grade that Milton Hershey completed before his mother took him out of school so that he could learn a trade?

READ LETTERS TO SANTA CLAUS

Let's face it. Santa gets a lot of mail. He can't possibly answer all those letters by himself. Thankfully, the small town of Santa Claus, Indiana, ensures that all those envelopes don't go unopened.

Stop by the Santa Claus Museum & Village to read through the current displays of actual letters sent to Santa from children (and adults) from around the country. Letters are rotated regularly and separated by decades. The first thing you'll note is the beautiful handwriting of children decades ago (not so much today). Letters vary from heartwarming to funny, bizarre, and even sad.

Guests can write their own letter to Santa in the nearby schoolhouse and get a special Santa Claus postmark at the town's post office. Also check out Santa's Candy Castle down the street. The biggest attraction in town is Holiday World, which is recognized as America's very first theme park. It also offers free parking and drinks with admission.

69 State Road 245
Santa Claus, IN 47579
812-544-2434
santaclausind.org

ROAD TRIP TRIVIA QUESTION #21

Today, the nonprofit organization Santa's Elves, Inc., and the Santa Claus Museum organize volunteers to answer all the children's letters that flood the Santa Claus, Indiana, post office during the holidays. On average, how many letters do they answer?

Columbiana,
Alabama
Oct. - 1940

Dear Santa Clause,
    I have been a very good big
girl this year. I haven't hit my 2
brothers over 1,350 times.
    Santa Clause I want a 1961
Cadillac and mother said I
could have the Lone Ranger's
horse "Silver" and Tonto if
possible.
    We won't have a fire in the
fireplace because I'm afraid you
might get burnt coming down it.
    Mother said she would leave
you some beer an a jar of Rattle-
snakes for your deer.
                    With hopes,
                    Sue

P.S. Hope you make it, not really you but
the Cadillac and especially "TonTo"
        "I just thought I would get my order in early"

TOUR WARNER BROTHERS STUDIO

The average American watches thirty-five hours of television each week, but most of us don't really know what all goes into producing those comedy shows or addicting dramas that consume big portions of our lives.

Warner Brothers Studio in Burbank, California, offers the absolute best behind-the-scenes look at movie and television production. You'll board a tram that takes you to the studio back lot for a one-of-a-kind tour. As production schedules change each day, there's no way to tell just what you'll see or where you'll get to go. The last time I took the tour I found myself on the sets of *Everybody Loves Raymond* and *Gilmore Girls* and walked the halls of the hit TV drama *ER*.

You'll see iconic movie sets and possibly run into a celebrity filming a new movie. Many popular TV shows are filmed at Warner Brothers, and you can obtain free tickets to be a member of the studio audience.

3400 Warner Blvd.
Burbank, CA 91505
877-492-8687
wbstudiotour.com

ROAD TRIP TRIVIA QUESTION #22
What do movie studios often use as "fake snow"
for those cold winter scenes?

HOW TO SEE A TV SHOW TAPING

Get Tickets!

All tickets to see television show tapings are absolutely free. Shows that air every day, such as game shows or daytime talk shows, are easiest to see. Tickets to popular sitcoms go fast. With few exceptions, tickets must be obtained online.

tvtickets.com

mytvtickets.com

tvtix.com

Getting There

In Los Angeles, most shows are taped at a handful of studios, including Warner Brothers and Paramount studios. It's important to remember that you bring a photo ID and arrive early, as they give out more tickets than seats available. You're typically not allowed to bring anything, including cellphones, into the studio with you.

What to Expect

You'll be amazed by what goes on behind the scenes during the taping of a TV show. Pay attention to everything going, from the writers to the cameras and how the sets are designed! It will almost certainly be freezing cold because of the hot lights used during taping. Each thirty-minute show could take five hours or more to tape, so plan for a long night.

SEE THE BEATLES' DRUMS
AT THE ROCK AND ROLL HALL OF FAME

The Rock and Roll Hall of Fame in Cleveland, Ohio, is the world's best and biggest collection of priceless archives related to the music industry. The Beatles certainly have one of the most important places in rock and roll history, revolutionizing the American music scene in what's often called "the British invasion."

Of all the incredible artifacts in the museum, be sure to see Ringo Starr's drum set. In February 1964, one of the biggest moments in American pop culture took place when the Beatles performed on the *Ed Sullivan Show*. That drum set was seen on TV in 60 percent of households in the country.

Displays are constantly changing to make each visit unique. One day you might see a "meat dress" worn by Lady Gaga, while another day you may see Roy Orbison's sunglasses or pieces of the plane that crashed killing Otis Redding.

1100 E. Ninth St.
Cleveland, OH 44114
216-781-7625
rockhall.com

ROAD TRIP TRIVIA QUESTION #23
What is the name of the disc jockey who coined
the phrase "rock and roll"?

FIND YOUR FAVORITE TOY
AT THE TOY HALL OF FAME

The Strong National Museum of Play in Rochester, New York, is one of the most underrated museums in the country. No matter your age, you'll see toys you played with as a child or perhaps toys that you always wanted. The original Monopoly board is a gem among the huge display of classic games from every generation. You'll see the first talking doll and the world's largest Erector set and test your memory with a touch-screen concentration game.

In 2002 the museum obtained the National Toy Hall of Fame from A.C. Gilbert's Discovery Village in Salem, Oregon. A state-of-the-art exhibit space pays homage to each of the inductees and has interactive displays. Recent toys inducted include the Rubber Duck, Barbie, Scrabble, and Frisbee.

Be sure to bring some extra dollars for video game tokens in the museum's video game collection. Play pinball, arcade games, and more!

One Manhattan Square Dr.
Rochester, NY 14607
585-263-2700
museumofplay.org

ROAD TRIP TRIVIA QUESTION #24
What is unique about the original Monopoly board that's on display at the Strong National Museum of Play?

BE A KID AGAIN AT
THE CHILDREN'S MUSEUM OF INDIANAPOLIS

The biggest children's museum in the country is hardly a place that's just for children. All ages love the exhibits and displays made up from the museum's 120,000-piece collection. From the moment you walk in and see the seventeen-foot replica of Bumblebee from the movie *Transformers,* you'll want to spend an entire day exploring.

The museum is brilliantly designed for families to interact and learn together. You can discuss dinosaurs with actual paleontologists on-site cleaning newly discovered fossils in the Dinosphere. Learn all about children who have made an impact in the world while visiting the permanent exhibit "The Power of Children: Making A Difference." Impressive displays tell the inspiring stories of Anne Frank, Ruby Bridges, and Ryan White.

Be sure to take note of the single-largest and complex Chihuly art piece called "Fireworks of Glass" while walking up to each of the museum's four floors.

3000 N. Meridian St
Indianapolis, IN 46208
800-820-6214
childrensmuseum.org

ROAD TRIP TRIVIA QUESTION #25
What superstar was last seen in concert at Indy's
Market Square Arena in 1977?

GET CULTURED AT
THE PHILBROOK MUSEUM OF ART

Step inside the former home of Waite Phillips that was donated to the city of Tulsa in 1938. Phillips, founder of the Phillips 66 oil company, lived in this 72-room mansion with his wife, Genevieve. The mansion is described as an Italian Renaissance villa that sits on twenty-three acres. Today, their gift to Tulsa is one of the finest art museums in the United States. Portions of the estate have been altered to accommodate the public, but much has remained the same from its days as a private residence.

The Philbrook collection encompasses American, European, Native American, Asian, African, and Modern art exhibits. Notable artists include Pablo Picasso, Giovanni Bellini, Georgia O'Keeffe, Rachel Whiteread, and Andrew Wyeth.

The property includes an elaborate garden that resembles Villa Lante, an estate near Rome designed by Giacomo Barozzi da Vignola in 1566. The gardens are a popular spot for photographs and weddings.

2727 S. Rockford Rd.
Tulsa, OK 74114
918-749-7941
philbrook.org

ROAD TRIP TRIVIA QUESTION #26
What is the name of the 75-foot statue located in Tulsa that honors oil workers? It is one of the tallest statues in the US.

SUN STUDIO:
HEAR ELVIS PRESLEY'S FIRST RECORDING

Tourists from around the world flock to Memphis each year to stand in the historic Sun Studio where Elvis was discovered and launched his career. While looking at the original sound-proofing tiles on the walls and ceiling, you'll have the chance to stand in the very spot where the future King of Rock and Roll stood as he made his singing debut. In fact, your tour will include audio of early studio sessions that will almost certainly give you goosebumps as you listen and look around in awe.

Recording pioneer Sam Phillips first opened the building as Memphis Recording Service in 1950.

Elvis wasn't the only music legend to record at Sun Studio. Johnny Cash, Carl Perkins, B.B. King, Roy Orbison, Charlie Rich, and Jerry Lee Lewis recorded there until the mid-1950s. The studio has since been used for recording sessions with such artists as Bonnie Raitt, Ringo Starr, and U2.

706 Union Ave.
Memphis, TN 38103
901-521-0664
sunstudio.com

ROAD TRIP TRIVIA QUESTION #27
On December 4, 1956, Elvis, Johnny Cash, Carl Perkins, and Jerry Lee Lewis had a jam session inside Sun Studio. What is the name of the popular musical that tells the story of that special evening?

IN THE NEIGHBORHOOD

Graceland
Take a tour through the former home of Elvis Presley.
You'll see his living room, the famous Jungle Room, and
the shaggy green carpet on the walls. Don't miss
the massive collection of golf records after touring the
home. Photographs are allowed inside, and an audio
headphone tour gives a general overview of the estate.

3717 Elvis Presley Blvd.
Memphis, TN 38116
901-332-3322
graceland.com

Beale Street
The famous American street is a bucket list item for most.
Home to shopping, dining, and, of course, drinking.

bealestreet.com

The Peabody Hotel
Be sure to watch the famous Peabody Ducks. For more
than ninety years, the Ducks have marched to the lobby
fountain each day at 11 a.m. and 5 p.m.

149 Union Ave.
Memphis, TN 38103
901-529-4000
peabodymemphis.com

CarrValley
CHEESE
www. carrvalleycheese.com

Owr e Cook r - 100 Years Cheese Making E
ONSIN OLD FASHIONED W

CARR V LEY
CHEESE OR
old
ore,
608.822.6

CARR VAL O
Fa
S 37
La Vall
608.986.2781

CARR VAL
CHEESE S
2831 P 160
Middl

Ch
Eagle
807 P
Sauk City, 3

CARR VALL
HEESE ST
 Broad
onsin W
.254.

, INC.

FOOD AND DRINK

EAT FRESH CHEESE CURDS
IN WISCONSIN

Folks in the Badger state do not play around when it comes to cheese. Although cheese curds have been duplicated all over the country, there's nothing quite like eating fresh cheese curds in Wisconsin.

They are available at many cheese factories all over the state, and the key is getting them "fresh." For best results, try them warm out of the bin at a factory. Fresh cheese curds have a kind of squeak when you bite into them. The most common seems to be the plain cheddar variety.

ROAD TRIP TRIVIA QUESTION #28
Madison, Wisconsin, is one of only two major American cities built on an isthmus. What's the other one?

Here are a few options for great cheese curds
while visiting Wisconsin:

Graze

Located on Capital Square in Madison
608-251-2700
grazemadison.com

Craftsman Table & Tap

6712 Frank Lloyd Wright Ave.
Middleton, WI 53562
craftsmantableandtap.com

Great Dane Pub & Brewing Company

123 E. Doty St.
Madison, WI 53703
608-284-0000
downtown.greatdanepub.com

Titletown Brewing Company

200 Dousman St.
Green Bay, WI 54303

AJ Bombers

1241 N. Water St.
Milwaukee, WI 53202
414-221-9999
hospitalitydemocracy.com

CATCH LOBSTER
IN MAINE

For many lifelong residents of Maine, fishing for lobster is just a regular part of life. Lobsters are harvested year-round in the state, with most caught between July and December when most are active. Lobsters are also harvested during the winter and early spring months, but in smaller numbers.

A fisherman uses colored buoys to mark each of his traps. Each trap catches a dramatically different number of lobsters, with many different variables at hand. The traps are usually hauled in at least once a week. Contrary to popular belief, lobsters aren't red until after you cook them. When alive, a lobster's shell is made up of many different types of pigments and appears green or brown. The heat from cooking destroys all of those pigments, giving the shell the red color.

On a guided boat tour, visitors have countless opportunities to get an up-close look at the entire process of catching lobsters.

lobsterfrommaine.com

ROAD TRIP TRIVIA QUESTION #29
True or false? Lobsters cry when you boil them.

TOUR BEN & JERRY'S ICE CREAM FACTORY

Ben & Jerry have been pleasing sweet tooths, mending broken hearts, and filling the cravings of pregnant women since 1978. After a $12,000 investment, the Vermont-based ice cream company began operating inside a renovated gas station. Today, its world headquarters in Waterbury is a popular tourist destination.

The company is best known for its clever flavor names, such as The Tonight Dough, Americone Dream, Chunky Monkey, Cherry Garcia, and Half Baked. Each tour lasts about thirty minutes and includes a free sample after an up-close look at the production process. Tickets are sold on a first come, first served basis each day.

After a short walk up the hill behind the factory, you'll find the Ben & Jerry's Flavor Graveyard, a cemetery for previous ice cream flavors that are no longer in circulation. Each headstone gives a description of the flavor and how it came to be.

1281 Waterbury-Stowe Rd.
Waterbury, VT 05676
benjerry.com

ROAD TRIP TRIVIA QUESTION #30
Before ice cream, what did Ben & Jerry originally plan to sell, but the equipment was too expensive?

HAVE FRIED CHICKEN
AT TWO SISTERS KITCHEN

It's a safe bet that you'll find a line from the front porch down onto the sidewalk when lunchtime rolls around at Two Sisters Kitchen in Jackson, Mississippi. The buffet sits inside an old house not far from the state capitol building and features that old-fashioned, down-home cooking you expect in this part of the South.

While fried chicken is the star of the show, other delicious items of interest include grits, succotash, carrots, green beans, and black-eyed peas. Don't you dare leave without trying some of their homemade bread pudding. The food is amazing, and the staff and surrounding atmosphere are quite welcoming. They are open every day for lunch except Saturday.

Perhaps a Yelp reviewer from Florida said it best: "If I was on death row, the night before my execution, this would be what I would have for my last meal."

707 N. Congress St.
Jackson, MS 39202
601-353-1180

ROAD TRIP TRIVIA QUESTION #31
Jackson is one of four US capitals named after US presidents.
What are the other three?

ENJOY A BEER
AT FROSTY BAR ON PUT-IN-BAY

Located in the heart of downtown Put-in-Bay, Frosty Bar has been serving generations of visitors to the island since 1956. It's tradition to have a cold beer served in its signature frosty beer mug! You'll find peanut shells crunching under your feet, tasty pizza baked fresh to order, and classic rock tunes from the jukebox. Native islanders, boaters, and day trippers alike flock to Frosty Bar for the beautiful view of DeRivera Park and the Put-in-Bay harbor.

Put-in-Bay is located on South Bass Island and accessible by ferry from mainland Ohio. Once on the island, you can walk or rent a golf cart for transportation. The area is known for its nightlife but is family friendly as well during the daytime hours.

Be sure to visit Kelleys Island while you're in the area for a slightly more peaceful and serene Lake Erie experience.

252 Delaware Ave.
Put-in-Bay, OH 43456
419-285-4741
frostys.com

ROAD TRIP TRIVIA QUESTION #32
Perry's Victory and International Peace Memorial at Put-in-Bay is currently the fourth tallest National Monument in the United States at 352 feet. What is the tallest?

TAKE A CHICAGO PIZZA TOUR

The average American eats more than forty pounds of pizza each year, making it a multibillion dollar industry in the US. Any pizza enthusiast would agree that ALL pizza is good, whether it's New York style or the thin-crust variety, but deep-dish pizza made famous in Chicago is something everyone must try at least once!

Chicago Pizza Tours is the perfect way to go around town and sample all the different varieties of pizza available in the Windy City. It's a great way to see Chicago, learn some history, and, most important, eat lots of pizza!

chicagopizzatours.com

ROAD TRIP TRIVIA QUESTION #33

The first deep-dish pizza was sold in 1943 at a Chicago restaurant that eventually became Pizzeria Uno. What type of food was the restaurant originally planning to sell?

Most folks know about Pizzeria Uno or Giordano's, but here are some other options for deep-dish pizza that you might enjoy even better:

Pizano's

Three dine-in locations in Chicago
pizanoschicago.com

Pequod's

2207 N. Clybourn Ave.
pequodspizza.com

Bartoli's

1995 W. Addison St.
bartolispizza.com

Bacino's

Two dine-in locations
bacinos.com

Exchequer

226 S. Wabash
exchequerpub.com

VISIT JACK DANIELS
IN LYNCHBURG, TENNESSEE

Back in 1886, Jasper Newton Daniels opened what would become the first registered distillery in the United States. While touring the property, guests quickly learn that the Jack Daniels product is just as popular as its history is interesting.

Over 300,000 visitors travel to Lynchburg each year and learn how a gregarious five-foot, two-inch man created the top-selling whiskey in the world. You'll also learn about Cave Spring Hollow and how its constant fifty-six degrees and clean, crisp water are particularly important in the unique Jack Daniels taste. Be sure to take note of the safe that killed him, too.

Here's a funny twist—you can't actually purchase Jack Daniels, even in the town that's become famous for it. Lynchburg is located in a dry county, meaning that the only legal purchase you can make is in the gift store. Even then, it's still illegal to taste it.

182 Lynchburg Hwy.
Lynchburg, TN 37352
931-759-6357
jackdaniels.com

ROAD TRIP TRIVIA QUESTION #34
What legendary American singer and performer was buried with a bottle of Jack Daniels?

HAVE SWEET TEA
IN THE SOUTH

How could sweet tea possibly taste better in the South than it does anywhere else in America? Perhaps it's for the same reason that a $10 plate of nachos tastes better at a baseball game than it does at home where it costs you nothing. Folks in the South will tell you that there's definitely a difference between "sweet tea" and "sweetened tea." Dumping sugar into a glass of iced tea does not make it sweet tea.

Can't wait to try Southern sweet tea? Try this recipe:

Boil one quart of cool filtered or bottled water, bringing to a full, rolling boil, and then turn off the heat. Steep Luzianne tea bags in the hot water for nine minutes. Gently squeeze bags of excess water and remove. Whisk in 1/2 cup sugar (or 1 cup for more sweet) and a pinch of baking soda until dissolved, and set aside. Fill pitcher with ice and carefully pour the hot tea concentrate over the ice. Stir well and pour over ice-filled glasses, garnishing with a sprig of mint leaves and a nice juicy slice of lemon. Savor. Makes two quarts.

ROAD TRIP TRIVIA QUESTION #35
In the movie *Steel Magnolias,* who defined sweet tea as "the house wine of the South"?

TRY ALL TYPES OF BBQ

Barbecue can be traced back to the early days of America, even before Christopher Columbus. The technique of cooking meat over indirect flames even dates back to early Native Americans, but to get a true sense of American barbecue, one must try a multitude of styles and meats from across the country.

Many purists will insist that their particular home region is "how barbecue is supposed to be." Whether you're eating pork in the Carolinas or beef in Texas, I believe variety is the spice of life, and you should try as many different styles of American BBQ as you can. Each region has its specialties, from chicken to lamb and sauces with everything from vinegar to mustard bases and various spices. Even side dishes change depending on where you are in the country.

BBQ can be enjoyed at many wonderful places, but here are a handful of my favorites.

ROAD TRIP TRIVIA QUESTION #36
What is the most popular American holiday for barbecuing in the US?

TASTIEST BBQ SUGGESTIONS

Central BBQ

2249 Central Ave.
Memphis, TN 38104
901-272-9377

Q39

1000 W. 39th St.
Kansas City, MO 64111
816-255-3753

Franklin Barbecue

900 E. Eleventh St.
Austin, TX 78702
512-653-1187

Pappy's Smokehouse

3106 Olive St.
Saint Louis, MO 63103
314-535-4340

Iron Star Urban Barbeque

3700 N. Shartel Ave
Oklahoma City, OK 73118
405-524-5925

SAMPLE LOUISIANA FOOD

A visit to Louisiana isn't complete until you've sampled the foods that help make this state such a unique and delightful part of the American experience.

Andouille
Cajun smoked sausage is made of pork meat and pork stomach. You'll find it often in gumbo and jambalaya.

Beignets
A deep-fried dough square generously sprinkled with powdered sugar.

Boudin
A sausage casing stuffed with rice, spices, and seafood. Usually crawfish or shrimp.

Crawfish
Sometimes called mudbugs. Crawfish boils are popular in the spring and early summer.

Gumbo
A thick soup or stew made with a roux base and chicken, seafood, or sausage.

Jambalaya
A one-pot meal of rice, vegetables, and meat. Vegetables used are celery, onion, and bell peppers. (AKA: "The Holy Trinity" in Cajun dishes.)

Mufaletta
A large, round sandwich made up of Italian-style meats, cheeses, and olive salad. Best place to get them is at Central Grocery in New Orleans's French Quarter.

Poboy (or poorboy)
A Louisiana sub sandwich, with French bread that's filled with shrimp, oysters, soft shell crab, ham and cheese, or maybe roast beef.

ROAD TRIP TRIVIA QUESTION #37
How many legs does a crawfish have?

HAVE A MINT JULEP
AT THE KENTUCKY DERBY

Sometimes things just go hand in hand. What would peanut butter be without jelly? How would Bert survive without Ernie? And what would a Kentucky Derby be without a mint julep? The official beverage of the world's biggest horse-racing event has been served at Churchill Downs since 1938.

It is always made with bourbon, lots of crushed or shaved ice, and fresh mint. Between the Derby and the Kentucky Oaks, about 120,000 mint juleps are served at the events each year in Louisville, Kentucky.

One misconception about the Kentucky Derby is that it's impossible to get a ticket unless you're rich or a celebrity. In fact, you can attend the event in many different ways in all price ranges. For around $1,000, you could wind up in a seat with a great view, or for closer to $5,000 you can get a standing-room-only ticket in the middle of the track. And, ladies, don't forget your fancy hat!

700 Central Ave.
Louisville, KY 40208
churchilldowns.com

ROAD TRIP TRIVIA QUESTION #38
The smallest field in Kentucky Derby history was back in 1892.
How many horses were in that race?

EAT THOMAS JEFFERSON ICE CREAM
AT MOUNT RUSHMORE

It's a popular myth that Thomas Jefferson introduced ice cream to America. It is true, however, that Jefferson had the first known recipe and helped make the cool treat popular in the States after serving it in his Washington home. That recipe is currently stored in the Library of Congress in DC.

Historians debate whether Jefferson should actually get credit for the recipe or if he just happened to be the one who thought to write it down. Either way it's a delicious treat served at Mount Rushmore in the Black Hills of South Dakota. The only difference in the current recipe from the one Jefferson wrote down in the 1780s? The milk is pasteurized.

After eating ice cream and posing for photos with the famous sculptures, be sure to visit the museum and see how Mount Rushmore was originally designed to look. Admission is free, but there is a parking charge. Save your receipt if you plan to come back again within a year.

13000 SD 244
Keystone, SD 57751
nps.gov/moru

ROAD TRIP TRIVIA QUESTION #39
Which of the presidents on Mount Rushmore was supposed to be located to the left of George Washington?

IN THE NEIGHBORHOOD

Custer State Park
A popular South Dakota destination for viewing buffalo
and antelope while enjoying the beauty of the Black Hills.

13329 US Hwy. 16A
Custer, SD 57730
605-255-4515
gfp.sd.gov/state-parks/directory/custer/

Crazy Horse Memorial
Started in 1948, the unfinished monument is under
construction on privately held land in the Black Hills.
It stands 564 feet high, making it the world's largest
mountain carving. The Crazy Horse museum features
a film and live Native American performances,
making it an interesting cultural stop.

12151 Ave. of the Chiefs
Crazy Horse, SD 57730
605-673-4681
crazyhorsememorial.org

Jewel Cave
The third-longest cave in the world.
Tours are offered year-round, weather permitting.

11149 US Hwy. 16, Building B12
Custer, SD 57730
605-673-8300
nps.gov/jeca

EXPLORE LITTLE ROCK'S RIVER MARKET DISTRICT

A friend of mine once advised me to steer clear of Little Rock, dismissing the state's capital city as a place with nothing to see or do. Thankfully, I didn't listen to that advice and now consider it one of my favorite Southern stops, with great people and plenty to experience.

Little Rock has been named a top food destination by numerous magazines and surveys in recent years. The River Market District has been important for making this town a hip place to hang out, work, and live. You can walk along the river and check out awesome sculptures, grab some fresh produce at the farmers market, and watch the bridges light up each night with bright, beautiful colors.

A $300 million riverfront development project brought the once desolate neighborhood back to life and now serves as a cultural center point for the city. Don't drive on past Little Rock or the River Market!

400 President Clinton Ave.
Little Rock, AR 72201
501-376-4781
rivermarket.info

ROAD TRIP TRIVIA QUESTION #40
Arkansas is the birthplace of what popular type of snack dip?
It was invented in 1935 by Blackie Donnelly,
owner of Mexico Chiquito Restaurant.

IN THE NEIGHBORHOOD

Museum of Discovery

Arkansas's premier science and technology center. Lots of fun, interactive exhibits that help teach all ages about everything from the human body to math and space.

500 President Clinton Ave. #150
Little Rock, AR 72201
501-396-7050
museumofdiscovery.org

Esse Purse Museum

The only museum in the United States dedicated to the history of purses through the decades. Exhibits showcase a variety of purses and a look at the contents you'd find in them at different points in American history.

1510 Main St.
Little Rock, AR 72202
501-916-9022
essepursemuseum.com

Arkansas River Lights

Every evening from dusk through dawn three Little Rock bridges are illuminated using thousands of high-efficiency LEDs, creating a dazzling light show over the Arkansas River.

River Market Dist.
400 President Clinton Ave.
Little Rock, AR 72201
arkansasriverlights.com

SPORTS AND RECREATION

VISIT COOPERSTOWN
IN OCTOBER

Fall is the absolute best time to visit this small upstate New York village. Made famous as the hometown of the National Baseball Hall of Fame, it's also ranked as one of the best places in America to view fall colors. As an added bonus, the crowds are generally smaller this time of the year. Time it right and you can be there during the World Series, which is extra special.

The experience inside baseball's most sacred destination doesn't disappoint. You'll see one-of-a-kind pieces, such as Stan Musial's locker or bats, balls, shoes, jerseys, and gloves used by the greatest players in baseball history. An excellent documentary is included with your admission that you'll view inside a theater designed like a baseball field. The best part of Cooperstown, however, is hearing stories and sharing memories with other baseball fans from around the world.

25 Main St.
Cooperstown, NY 13326
607-547-7200
baseballhall.org

ROAD TRIP TRIVIA QUESTION #41
What movie starring Tom Hanks and Geena Davis was filmed at Doubleday Field, just around the corner from the Baseball Hall of Fame?

Stan Musial's Locker

ATTEND THE INDY 500

If you're a fan of racing, this is probably already on your list. If you're like me and know pretty much nothing about the sport, trust me, do not skip over this one. The Indy 500 and the pageantry around it are nothing short of incredible. I cannot overemphasize how glad I am that I decided to attend the ninety-ninth running of the Indy 500 despite knowing none of the drivers or much else.

The sights and the sounds of these cars flying around the track at more than two hundred miles per hour are simply amazing. The Indianapolis Motor Speedway is beyond huge at 560 acres, something that doesn't always compute while watching on television. Knowing you're sharing the experience with more than 300,000 people is also mind boggling. The IMS museum is really cool too.

Oh, and wait until you see folks parking their cars on front lawns of neighborhood houses. It's wild.

4790 W. Sixteenth St.
Indianapolis, IN 46222
317-492-8500
indianapolismotorspeedway.com

ROAD TRIP TRIVIA QUESTION #42
Which of the following could fit inside the Indianapolis Motor Speedway? Churchill Downs, Vatican City, Yankee Stadium, the Roman Coliseum, or the Rose Bowl?

IN THE NEIGHBORHOOD

Conner Prairie Interactive History Park
A Smithsonian affiliate history park located just
outside of Indianapolis in nearby Fishers, Indiana.
Fantastic place to take the children.

13400 Allisonville Rd.
Fishers, IN 46038
connerprairie.org

Love Sculpture
The original LOVE sculpture is located at the
Indianapolis Museum of Art. The sculpture has been
replicated by artist Robert Indiana in such places as
New York City and Philadelphia.

4000 Michigan Rd.
Indianapolis, IN 46208
imamuseum.org

Action Duckpin Bowl
Just like regular bowling except the ball is much
smaller and you get three throws instead of two.
The Fountain Square location is one of the few duckpin
bowling alleys left in the United States.

1105 Prospect St.
Indianapolis, IN 46203
fountainsquareindy.com

International Orangutan Center
This award-winning, one-of-a-kind facility is located inside
the Indianapolis Zoo. Guests can see these animals up close
and watch them explore their state-of-the-art habitat, and
the orangutans have an opportunity to interact as well.

1200 W. Washington St.
Indianapolis, IN 46222
indianapoliszoo.com

ATTEND THE MASTERS GOLF TOURNAMENT

Getting a ticket to watch the Masters golf tournament may be just about as tough as snagging a seat at the Super Bowl, but it's the rich, long-standing traditions that make this such a great event and something special to witness in person.

The Masters is the only major golf tournament played in the same location each year. It's also the only time the general public can visit the course, as it's a private club with new members welcomed by invitation only.

Even if you're not a huge golf fan, you'll be able to appreciate the gorgeous scenery and, most important, the incredibly cheap concession prices. Despite being one of the most coveted tickets in sports, the food prices at the Masters haven't budged much from what they were back in the 1970s. In 2016 soft drinks were $1.50, while beer was only $3. A club sandwich will set you back $2.50, while their famous pimiento cheese sandwich costs $1.50.

2604 Washington Rd.
Augusta, GA 30904
masters.com

ROAD TRIP TRIVIA QUESTION #43
What are all the holes on the golf course named after?

SING "SWEET CAROLINE"
AT FENWAY PARK

Fenway Park, home of the Boston Red Sox, is the oldest Major League Baseball stadium in the US. First opened in 1912 (just five days after the sinking of the Titanic), the legendary sports venue has seen its share of historical moments and legendary players—Babe Ruth, Cy Young, Ted Williams, and Carl Yastrzemski, to name just a few. Fenway's "Green Monster" is its most recognized feature, even though the famous outfield wall wasn't painted green until 1947.

Besides watching a game in America's oldest baseball stadium, you can also participate in a relatively new tradition. Since 2002, Neil Diamond's hit song "Sweet Caroline" plays on the loud speakers for a fun sing-a-long before the bottom of the eighth inning. If you can't catch a game when you're in Boston, be sure to take a tour of the stadium.

4 Yawkey Way
Boston, MA 02215
877-733-7699
boston.redsox.mlb.com

ROAD TRIP TRIVIA QUESTION #44
Fenway is the oldest baseball stadium in America.
What two MLB stadiums are next in line?

GROS VENTRE DUDE RANCH
IN JACKSON HOLE, WY

Experience what American life was like for early explorers of the Wild West by spending time at the Gros Ventre River Ranch. Even with little or no previous experience in horse riding, guests can enjoy soaking up incredible views while snug in the saddle. In addition to channeling your inner cowboy (or cowgirl), you can parachute off a mountain, go paddleboarding, or go rock climbing.

Not far from the ranch you'll find the Snake River as it winds through Grand Teton National Park. It's known as one of the best floating rivers in the country. Yellowstone National Park is also nearby. The scenery is spectacular and a perfect reminder of (or introduction to) America's vast and gorgeous natural landscapes. While at Gros Ventre, you can stay in a log cabin while dining on family-style meals in the resort's main lodge. It's a perfect setting for families or large groups.

307-733-4318
grosventreriverranch.com

ROAD TRIP TRIVIA QUESTION #45
A ribbon is tied to a horse's tail to indicate that it's prone to kick.
What color is that ribbon?

WATCH A FOOTBALL GAME
AT LAMBEAU FIELD

It's hard to argue that the relationship between the Green Bay Packers franchise and its fans is one of the most special in all of professional sports. Named in tribute of longtime coach Curly Lambeau, the home turf of the Packers is often called the Frozen Tundra after a famous game in 1967 when the entire field was frozen.

Lambeau is the oldest field in the NFL and sits at an elevation of 640 feet above sea level. Season tickets have been sold out since 1960, and the waiting list extends beyond 100,000 people. It is the only publicly owned major sports franchise in the US.

The best part of the Lambeau experience is the fans themselves. It's not uncommon for hundreds of fans to volunteer their time just for the opportunity to shovel snow at the stadium. Recent stadium improvements include a massive fifty-foot replica of the Lombardi Trophy and self-serve beer machines.

1265 Lombardi Ave.
Green Bay, WI 54304
packers.com

ROAD TRIP TRIVIA QUESTION #46
Since 1985, what song has been played inside Lambeau Field when the Green Bay Packers score a touchdown?

TAKE A RIVERBOAT TOUR
ON THE MISSISSIPPI RIVER

The Mississippi River is the fourth longest river in the world and has been the setting for many of America's historic chapters. Steamboats were used to deliver goods and help in the expansion of the American West. Mark Twain's most famous works were inspired along the river's shores in Hannibal, Missouri.

Today, you can still enjoy views from up and down the Mississippi River from vessels of all sizes. The Belle of Louisville is currently the oldest operating steamboat in the country and offers regular tours. Other replica or restored steamboats and paddleboats operate from towns along the river, with a unique perspective of how important the mighty Mississippi was in their town's development.

Here are some suggestions of places to see the river up close:

Dubuque, IA
dubuqueriverrides.com

Louisville, KY
belleoflouisville.org

Memphis, TN
memphisriverboats.net

St. Louis, MO
gatewayarch.com

St. Paul, MN
riverrides.com

Tunica, MS
tunicariverpark.com

New Orleans, LA
steamboatnatchez.com

Alton, IL
greatriverroad.com

ROAD TRIP TRIVIA QUESTION #47
The Mississippi River touches ten different states from north to south. Which of these states has the largest population?

HAVE A PICNIC
AT FALLS PARK IN GREENVILLE, SC

Falls Park is one of the most beautiful green spaces in the entire country. Nestled in the downtown area of Greenville, South Carolina, it serves as an oasis for residents and visitors to gather, walk, run, and enjoy nature.

With the relaxing sound of waterfalls, the sight of bright green grass, and 20,000 plants and flowers, there's no better setting for a picnic in the park.

Falls Park has won numerous awards and worldwide recognition for its design and contributions to the community. The city is also home to the Swamp Rabbit Trail, a twenty-mile walking and biking trail that runs along former railroad lines bordering the Reedy River and connects Greenville neighborhoods with downtown.

There's no admission fee, and free two-hour parking is available on the street.

864-467-4355
greenvillesc.gov

ROAD TRIP TRIVIA QUESTION #48

The historic Westin Poinsett Hotel in Greenville is featured in what 2008 George Clooney film, where his character drives up on a motorcycle?

GO FISHING
IN THE KENAI RIVER

Home to the world's largest sport-caught king salmon, the Kenai River is unsurprisingly Alaska's most renowned fishing destination. While more than thirty species of fish call "The Kenai" home, the river is best known for its prolific salmon and trout populations.

Silt from the Kenai River's glacier-fed headwaters gives the river a distinctive turquoise appearance, which increases in intensity as you move upriver from the Cook Inlet toward Kenai Lake, a trip of approximately eighty-two miles. The river winds through a small collection of communities and a wide variety of terrain, ranging from wetlands to forests and pristine mountainsides punctuated with feeder streams and springs.

While many visitors limit their experience to road-accessible portions of the river, a whole other world of scenery and fishing opportunity awaits those willing to invest the modest time and resources needed to access more remote areas.

Kenai River Sportfishing Association
907-262-8588
krsa.com

ROAD TRIP TRIVIA QUESTION #49
Fifty-two percent of Alaskans are what gender?
It's the highest percentage of any state.

HIKE
IN JOSHUA TREE NATIONAL PARK

Two desert ecosystems merge within this national park that was first established in 1994. Over a million visitors a year explore Joshua Tree to get a firsthand glimpse of unique plants and wildlife, including bighorn sheep, desert iguanas, and roadrunners.

Hiking is especially popular in the park, with trails showing awesome rock formations and complex variations of desert mosaic. Rock climbing is also wildly popular here, with more than 4,500 established climbing routes according to the National Park Service. Bird-watching is also a popular activity, with more than 240 bird species in the area.

So why is it named Joshua Tree National Park? According to legend, Mormon immigrants saw trees with limbs stretching outward as they arrived and named them Joshua trees after the biblical figure. The trees are an important habitat to many forms of wildlife that live within the park.

Joshua Tree Visitor Center
6554 Park Blvd.
Joshua Tree, CA 92252
760-367-5500
nps.gov/jotr

ROAD TRIP TRIVIA QUESTION #50
What two deserts make up Joshua Tree National Park?

DRIVE
THROUGH THEODORE ROOSEVELT NATIONAL PARK

This park is named after America's thirty-second President, Roosevelt, who fell in love with the area after hunting bison in 1883. Visitors can still see his maltese cross cabin, which was fully restored back in 2000. The most popular way to see a good mix of scenery and wildlife is by car on the Scenic Loop Drive. While on the thirty-six-mile loop through the south unit of the park, you'll see everything from prairie dogs to wild horses.

Other sights include the Elkhorn Ranch where the former president had his "home ranch" in the state. Painted Canyon Visitor Center provides a beautiful panoramic view of the badlands. Be sure to stop in the town of Medora for a folksy Western welcome to North Dakota. The Medora Musical is a popular tradition here each summer.

Always be aware of road conditions here in the winter months, as traveling can be unsafe.

315 Second Ave.
Medora, ND 58645
701-623-4466
nps.gov/thro

ROAD TRIP TRIVIA QUESTION #51
What river runs through Theodore Roosevelt National Park?
It's the only aquatic environment in the park that can support fish.

SEARCH FOR DIAMONDS
IN ARKANSAS

Find a diamond at Crater of Diamonds State Park and you can keep it! Sound too good to be true? It isn't!

For less than $10, you can spend an entire day searching a 37½-acre field that was once a diamond-bearing volcanic crater. A 40.23-carat white diamond was found here in 1924, which to date is the largest diamond ever found in the US. Other big finds include a 6.72-carat diamond in 1997 and a 6.35-carat diamond in 2006. The average diamond found is about one quarter of a carat. You can find three colors: clear white, yellow, and brown. If you find a diamond, the park staff will identify and certify it for you on the spot!

The park is open year-round, and guests can camp as well as rent equipment for digging. Consider bringing your own bucket, knee pads, and a small shovel.

209 State Park Rd.
Murfreesboro, AR 71958
870-285-3113
craterofdiamondsstatepark.com

ROAD TRIP TRIVIA QUESTION #52
What is the official state slogan/motto of Arkansas?

TAKE A HOT AIR BALLOON RIDE
OVER ALBUQUERQUE, NM

There's a reason that Albuquerque is the world capital of ballooning. The views from above the New Mexico terrain and the Sandria Mountains go beyond breathtaking, particularly at sunrise.

Ballooning has been a popular activity in Albuquerque for decades. Countless operators and companies can take you up in the air at just about any time of the year. If you're not quite brave enough to hop in the basket, the annual balloon festival happens in October and features around five hundred balloons. Consider joining the 750,000 people who attend each year to see the popular balloon glow and other events. The Albuquerque International Balloon Fiesta is said to be the most photographed event in the world.

Albuquerque is also home to the world's largest balloon museum dedicated to the history and culture of ballooning.

Anderson-Abruzzo International Balloon Museum
9201 Balloon Museum Dr.
Albuquerque, NM 87113
505-768-6020

Hot air balloon operators: visitalbuquerque.org/things-to-do/air/ballooning

ROAD TRIP TRIVIA QUESTION #53
True or false? In 1783, a rooster, a duck, and a sheep were the very first hot air balloon passengers?

WALK UNDERNEATH
THE NEW RIVER GORGE BRIDGE

The New River Gorge Bridge in Lansing, West Virginia, is the highest vehicle-carrying bridge in America at 876 feet. It was completed in 1977 with a type of steel called COR-TEN that has a rust-like appearance that never requires painting. Directly under the portion of the bridge used for vehicular traffic is a small, steel walkway. For a fee, you can do the "Bridge Walk," which takes you 1.25 miles across the two-foot wide walkway while secured to a safety line overhead. It can be windy and as much as ten degrees cooler under the bridge, so dress appropriately. Reservations are required.

Once a year the entire bridge shuts down for Bridge Day weekend, where folks can walk onto the bridge itself and enjoy activities to celebrate its initial opening. Each year adventurists also take part in parachuting off the bridge into the New River Gorge below.

304-574-1300
bridgewalk.com

ROAD TRIP TRIVIA QUESTION #54
Don Knotts, the actor best known for his role on *The Andy Griffith Show,* was born in West Virginia. What city was his hometown?

GO KAYAKING
IN THE EVERGLADES

While sharing some of my ideas for the book, a friend seemed puzzled when I suggested that kayaking in the Florida Everglades should be one of my 100 ideas. "You can actually kayak in there?" he asked. Absolutely.

Many people think of the Everglades as a bit of a forbidden ecosystem that only people with some sort of death wish visit. Actually, you have many opportunities to explore, and the best way is by kayak. It's also best done with an experienced guide who knows the terrain and can get you up close (safely) to some of the park's wildlife. You can expect to see manatees, sea turtles, dolphins, and probably an alligator.

The best time to visit is also the busiest time of the year. The first few months of the year are not nearly as hot and humid, and the bugs aren't quite as bad.

800-860-1472
evergladesareatours.com

877-567-0679
evergladesadventures.com

ROAD TRIP TRIVIA QUESTION #55
Are the Everglades a habitat for alligators or crocodiles?

RIDE THE COMET BOBSLED
AT UTAH OLYMPIC PARK

Park City, Utah, hosted the 2002 Winter Olympics, and even though the games are long over, Utah Olympic Park is still full of excitement! Guests can experience the feats of Olympians, following in their footsteps while climbing, sliding, and hiking. The 389-acre park is open year-round. The venue houses six Nordic ski jumps and a 750,000-gallon training pool.

The biggest adventure is a ride on the Winter Comet Bobsled that takes the same track Olympic bobsled teams used in 2002. You'll ride with a professional pilot and navigate fifteen curves at speeds of more than sixty mph while experiencing more than three times the force of gravity. If you can't make it during the winter months, an improvised bobsled (with wheels) provides a similar experience in the summer.

Be sure to visit the 2002 Olympic Winter Games Museum. Admission to the museum and parking are free.

3419 Olympic Pkwy.
Park City, UT 84098
435-658-4200
utaholympiclegacy.org

ROAD TRIP TRIVIA QUESTION #56
What country won the most medals in the 2002 Winter Olympics?

ZIP LINE UNDERGROUND
IN LOUISVILLE

It's one thing to take a zip line over trees or water, but how about a ride in the dark over canyons in a man-made cave? The Louisville Mega Cavern is the only place in the world where you can zip line underground, and it's an awesome experience. The cavern was mined from the early 1930s to the early 1970s. It's now privately owned.

Once suited up, you'll wear a hard hat with a flashlight and zip across several deep, dark canyons and cross several bridges that look like something out of an Indiana Jones movie (safely, of course).

The cavern includes seventeen miles of passageways and also features a bike park, aerial ropes course, and tram tour. The Mega Cavern is most popular locally for its Christmas light display, where cars drive through a thirty-minute light presentation that includes more than two million lights.

1841 Taylor Ave.
Louisville, KY 40213
877-614-6342
louisvillemegacavern.com

ROAD TRIP TRIVIA QUESTION #57
What major Louisville tourist attraction sits directly above the Mega Cavern?

IN THE NEIGHBORHOOD

Louisville Slugger Factory & Museum

800 W. Main St.
Louisville, KY 40202
877-775-8443
sluggermuseum.com

Muhammad Ali Center

144 N. Sixth St.
Louisville, KY 40202
502-584-9254
alicenter.org

Colonel Sanders Gravesite

Cave Hill Cemetery
701 Baxter Ave.
Louisville, KY 40204

Evan Williams Bourbon Experience

528 W. Main St.
Louisville KY 40202
502-272-2611
evanwilliams.com

RIDE A MULE
INTO THE GRAND CANYON

It's truly one of the great wonders of the world, and a photo doesn't do it justice. Neither does making the trip all the way to the Grand Canyon only to look over the edge and hop back into your car.

A ride into the canyon on a mule is the most adventurous and memorable way to experience your visit. If the thought of riding an animal on narrow pathways isn't for you, consider a ride along the edge of the canyon.

If you're physically able, even a short hike into the canyon is worth your effort. Winter is the best time to visit, as the crowds are smaller, and if you're lucky you'll see it covered in snow. The south rim is open year-round. Be sure to take plenty of water, food to snack on, and good hiking shoes. The elevation will certainly affect your body, so don't hike too far down if you're not experienced.

888-297-2757
grandcanyonlodges.com

ROAD TRIP TRIVIA QUESTION #58
How many deaths have occurred at the Grand Canyon as a result of mule rides since they started in 1887?

Snow-covered tracks of the Grand Canyon Railway

Gateway to the Blues Museum—
Tunica, MS (page 116)

The Louisiana State Capitol Building—
Baton Rouge, LA (page 108)

Covered Bridge—Madison County, IA (page 106)

The Munger House at Old Cowtown—Wichita, KS (page 9)

Creating the Game We Kn...
Charles D...

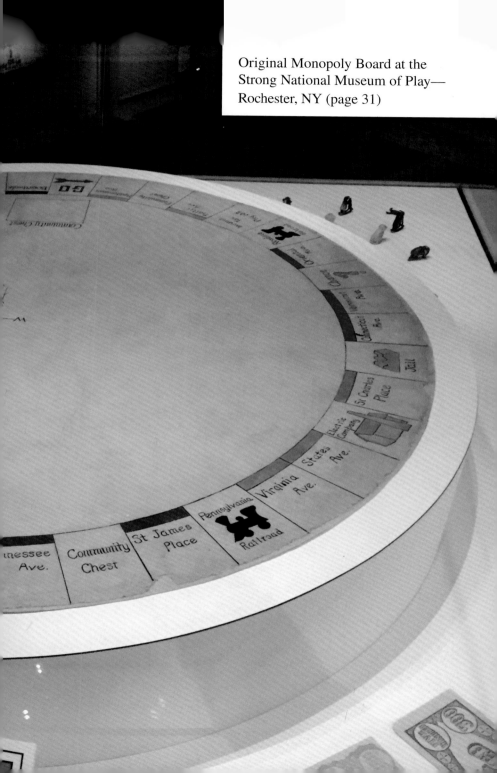

Original Monopoly Board at the Strong National Museum of Play—Rochester, NY (page 31)

Dome of the Old Courthouse—St. Louis, MO (page 21)

DEDICATED
TO THE CHILDREN OF THE WORLD
IN
MEMORY OF AN UNDYING LOVE
DEC 25 1935   Carl A Barrett

Fox Theatre—St. Louis, MO (page 22)

PHOTO OPS

THE HOLLYWOOD SIGN

The most recognized symbol of Southern California is the Hollywood sign that sits atop Mount Lee, the highest point in Los Angeles. The sign with its forty-five-foot letters was built in 1923 to promote a local real estate development called Hollywoodland. By 1949, the Hollywood Chamber of Commerce took ownership of the sign, dropping the "L-A-N-D" to promote the city instead of the development.

Because the sign was in serious need of repair, nine celebrities sponsored one letter each to pay for restoration. *Playboy* magazine founder Hugh Hefner led the effort along with Gene Autry, Alice Cooper, Andy Williams, and others. Each donated $27,777.77 for a total of $250,000. It is no longer legally possible to get next to the sign, but a couple of options are available to grab that Hollywood sign photo.

For the best photos, the closest you can get (by car) is on Canyon Lake Drive near the Hollywood Reservoir. On Beachwood Canyon Drive at Glen Holly, you can find the original entrance to Hollywoodland and a clear view for a photo. You should plan on walking to these locations, as parking is not permitted in most areas with close, clear views of the sign. Be aware of traffic and respectful of locals who live nearby.

hollywoodsign.org

ROAD TRIP TRIVIA QUESTION #59

The Hollywood sign is no longer lit up at night as it was originally. In fact, only one time since 1949 has the sign been illuminated. What was happening in 1984 that caused officials to light it up?

TOM SAWYER'S FENCE

America's most cherished author grew up in the small Mississippi River town of Hannibal, Missouri. Today, visitors can see firsthand the sights and sounds that inspired many of Mark Twain's famous stories. You can step inside his boyhood home as well as the homes of Becky Thatcher and Huckleberry Finn. A museum gallery and interpretive center tells the story of how Samuel Clemens went from just another boy living along the river to a prized author and larger-than-life figure of American culture.

Pose for a photo in front of the famous whitewashed fence described in the classic book *The Adventures of Tom Sawyer*. A bucket of paintbrushes is nearby to re-create the moment Tom talked his friends and neighbors into painting the fence. Be sure to see the statue of Tom Sawyer and Huck Finn, tour the Mark Twain cave, and take a ride on a paddleboat up and down the river.

415 N. Main St.
Hannibal, MO 63401
573-221-9010
visithannibal.com

ROAD TRIP TRIVIA QUESTION #60
What well-known Titanic survivor and influential women's rights advocate was also from the town of Hannibal?

STAND ON TOP OF STONE MOUNTAIN

Standing 825 feet above Atlanta, Georgia, is the top of Stone Mountain, with awesome visuals of the downtown skyline and views of the Appalachian Mountains. You'll hop aboard a high-speed Swiss cable car (an experience in its own right) all the way to the highest point before exiting and wandering around the surface of the mountaintop. Surrounding the bottom of the mountain is Stone Mountain Park, a theme park with rides, attractions, and shopping.

On the side of Stone Mountain, you'll see the massive Confederate Memorial Carving that depicts Jefferson Davis, Robert E. Lee, and Stonewall Jackson. The entire surface is more than three acres in size. The original sculptor, Gutzon Borglum, left the project in 1925 after a dispute with the management in charge of the carving. Borglum went on to carve a little project known as Mount Rushmore.

Don't miss the laser light show that runs each evening. Get a seat on the grass early, especially in summer.

100 Robert E. Lee Blvd.
Stone Mountain, GA 30083
800-401-2407
stonemountainpark.com

ROAD TRIP TRIVIA QUESTION #61
More than sixty-five streets in the Atlanta metro area include what word in their name?

IN THE NEIGHBORHOOD

Ebenezer Baptist Church
Where Dr. Martin Luther King Jr. was a pastor until his death in 1968. Have a seat in one of the pews and hear one of his recorded sermons in the sanctuary. His final resting place is right down the street.

450 Auburn Ave. NE
Atlanta, GA 30331
404-331-5190

World of Coca-Cola
The world headquarters of the soft drink giant offers tours and a complete Coca-Cola experience, including a taste-testing room to sample Coke products from around the world.

121 Baker St. NW
Atlanta, GA 30313
404-676-5151
worldofcoca-cola.com

Center for Puppetry Arts
A fun and informative look at the history of puppets, including a popular Jim Henson gallery that includes rotating displays of the original Muppet characters from *The Muppet Show, Sesame Street,* and *Fraggle Rock.*

1404 Spring St. NW
Atlanta, GA 30309
404-873-3391
puppet.org

KANSAS CITY FOUNTAINS

Kansas City is known for having the most fountains of any city in the United States and is only second to Rome worldwide. In the late 1800s, most fountains were used for practical purposes, such as keeping horses hydrated. Today, they simply add beauty to buildings and neighborhoods. A group called the City of Fountains Foundation was established in 1973 to raise money for upkeep of the historic fountains. A Hallmark executive named Harold Rice started the effort after a trip to Rome, where he saw many of the fountains there in bad condition. He didn't want the same thing to happen in Kansas City. The foundation's website has a map with locations of nearly all area fountains.

The Kansas City Parks & Recreation Department maintains forty-seven of these fountains, while others are privately owned and operated. It's fun to drive around town and see how many of the nearly two hundred fountains you can find.

kcfountains.com

ROAD TRIP TRIVIA QUESTION #62
The oldest fountain in Kansas City is located inside what museum?

IN THE NEIGHBORHOOD

National World War I Museum & Memorial

2 Memorial Dr.
Kansas City, MO 64108
816-888-8100
theworldwar.org

Negro Leagues Baseball Museum

1616 E. Eighteenth St.
Kansas City, MO 64108
816-221-1920
nlbm.com

National Museum of Toys & Miniatures

5235 Oak St.
Kansas City, MO 64112
816-235-8000
toyandminiaturemuseum.org

Hallmark Visitors Center

2450 Grand Blvd.
Kansas City, MO 64108
hallmarkvisitorscenter.com

Arabia Steamboat Museum

400 Grand Blvd.
Kansas City, MO 64106
816-471-1856
1856.com

WELCOME TO FABULOUS LAS VEGAS SIGN

You can't visit Sin City without a stop at the famous Las Vegas welcome sign. While one side welcomes you with a reminder to "drive carefully," the other side invites you to "come back soon." Initially, the legendary sign built in 1959 was placed in a busy section of town with limited access for visitors seeking a photo op. Today, a small parking lot is nearby that makes it much safer to access.

The sign is not only on the National Register of Historic Places, but it's also solar powered. The iconic Vegas symbol was designed by Betty Willis, an employee of the Western Neon Company, for a cost of $4,000. (She also designed the signs for the famous Moulin Rouge Hotel.)

To snap your photo, you must be heading south on Las Vegas Boulevard. You'll see the sign located just south of the Mandalay Bay Hotel & Casino. If you're headed in the other direction, you'll have to make a U-turn past the sign.

ROAD TRIP TRIVIA QUESTION #63

Who once stayed at the Desert Inn so long that he was asked to leave? Instead, he just bought the entire hotel.

GENERAL SHERMAN TREE

Located in the Sequoia and Kings Canyon National Park near Visalia, California, the General Sherman Tree is the largest tree in the world. It stands an astounding 275 feet high and is more than 36 feet wide at the base. By volume, it is the largest known living single-stem tree.

Two trails are found within the park that will get you to the General Sherman Tree. (You'll see the sign in front of it.) On the main trail, plan to walk about half a mile to reach the tree. The walk back will be uphill. The park service does offer a free shuttle in the summer and early fall. While tempting, don't stand under the tree or touch it, as its shallow root system is fragile.

In 1937 the park lost a giant 225-foot sequoia tree when it fell across a park road. Crews cut an eight-foot-tall, seventeen-foot-wide tunnel through its trunk that you can still drive through today.

559-565-3341
nps.gov/seki

ROAD TRIP TRIVIA QUESTION #64
In theory, how many miles of standard-size lumber planks could the trunk of the Sherman Tree be turned into?

COVERED BRIDGES
IN MADISON COUNTY, IOWA

The 1995 film *The Bridges of Madison County* made the area's covered bridges among the most popular in America. In the late nineteenth century, nineteen covered sections were built to protect the heavy and costly beams of actual bridges. (It was cheaper to repair the roof of the covered section than the bridge itself.) The film that stars Clint Eastwood and Meryl Streep made the remaining six bridges known to the world, and to this day tourists from across the globe stop through Madison County, Iowa, to see them.

All but one of the covered bridges are listed on the National Register of Historic Places. Each fall the Madison County Covered Bridge Festival takes place, where visitors celebrate all the red-and-white historic bridges. The Roseman Covered Bridge is supposedly haunted. Legend says that an escaped prisoner caught on the bridge by police rose up through the roof and vanished.

All the bridges are accessible and free of charge to see.

madisoncounty.com

ROAD TRIP TRIVIA QUESTION #65
What famous film star was born in Madison County?
His birth home and a museum celebrating his life and career
are in the town of Winterset.

THE LOUISIANA STATE CAPITOL BUILDING
IN BATON ROUGE

The nation's tallest capitol building is located in Baton Rouge, Louisiana. It took just over a year to build the thirty-four-story building that stands 450 feet high. The building was a vision of former governor Huey Long that came to life in 1932. Oddly enough, the capitol building is also where Governor Long was assassinated in 1935. Visitors can take a self-guided tour of the building and see both House and Senate chambers in addition to the observation deck on the twenty-seventh floor. The deck offers a great view of downtown Baton Rouge and the Mississippi River.

Be sure to take note of two odd displays within the building. First, bullet holes still exist in the wall, across from the governor's elevator, from the day when Governor Long was shot. Also, look up when you step into the Senate Chamber. There's a pencil in the ceiling that's been hanging there since 1970 after a bomb exploded.

900 N. Third St.
Baton Rouge, LA 70802
225-342-7317
visitbatonrouge.com

ROAD TRIP TRIVIA QUESTION #66
What does "Baton Rouge" mean in French?

BIG TEX
AT THE STATE FAIR OF TEXAS

Big Tex is the most iconic symbol of America's largest state fair, the State Fair of Texas. At fifty-five feet tall, Tex looks out over the millions of visitors who spill into the fairgrounds each fall. "Tex" was actually "Santa" when first built. The idea was to promote holiday spending by a local chamber of commerce. Two years later the statue was sold and turned into a giant cowboy for the State Fair. His appearance has been altered over the years, even animating his face and adding sounds so that he speaks to the crowd.

In 2012 an electrical fire caused Big Tex to go up in flames on the last weekend of the fair. The following year a new Big Tex was unveiled to the public. The latest version cost $500,000 and has new framework that can withstand a wind of one hundred mph.

The State Fair of Texas welcomes more than three million visitors each year.

bigtex.com

ROAD TRIP TRIVIA QUESTION #67
Big Tex's outfit usually lasts about three seasons before having to be changed. What brand of denim clothing does Big Tex wear for his shirt and pants?

NIAGARA FALLS

Many natural wonders in America aren't given justice in photographs or videos. Niagara Falls is one of those sights that simply cannot be captured by film, but we certainly have to try. The culmination of three great waterfalls—Horseshoe, American, and Bridal Veil—makes up the jaw-dropping visuals of Niagara Falls. Despite myths, it does not freeze, even in the coldest of winters.

Sadly, the environment surrounding Niagara Falls (on the American side) has become a huge tourist trap that makes the experience a bit less inspiring. Once you're inside the park, though, and see what 750,000 gallons of water a second gushing over cliffs looks like . . . Wow! The view of Niagara Falls is different from the Canadian side and definitely worth a look. You can walk across the Rainbow Bridge and take photos as long as you have a valid passport.

Niagara Falls State Park is the oldest state park in the US.

716-278-1796
niagara-usa.com

ROAD TRIP TRIVIA QUESTION #68
Four of the five Great Lakes drain into the Niagara River.
Name the four lakes.

THE HOOVER DAM

Each year seven million visitors witness this engineering marvel built during the Great Depression. Unemployed Americans flocked to Nevada for the chance to work on the project. In total, more than 21,000 people wound up having a hand in constructing Hoover Dam. Officially, ninety-six people died during construction. Oddly enough, Herbert Hoover became so unpopular as president that he wasn't even invited to the dam's dedication ceremony. Seventeen turbines generate power for 1.3 million homes in California, Arizona, and Nevada.

While visiting, you'll get great views of the Colorado River and Lake Mead while having the opportunity to venture into lesser-seen parts of the dam on an official tour. Tickets are available for tours on a first-come basis but are not recommended for people who suffer from claustrophobia. For photos, use the observation deck at the top of the visitors center, or locate one of the interpretive stations within the dam's secured zone.

702-494-2517
www.usbr.gov/lc/hooverdam

ROAD TRIP TRIVIA QUESTION #69
What comedy movie made fun of the Hoover Dam tour when actor Randy Quaid asked the tour guide, "Where can I get some damn bait?"

THE STATUE OF LIBERTY

Liberty Enlightening the World, or as most of us know it, the Statue of Liberty, was a gift from the people of France. She stands 306 feet high with a thirty-five-foot waist size. On October 28, 1886, the statue was dedicated with President Grover Cleveland on hand. In the 1980s, the statue underwent a major renovation from top to bottom by using the world's largest freestanding scaffold.

A small number of people can climb the 354 stairs to the top of the statue each day. The park service only allows groups of ten for each tour. Reservations can be made up to a year in advance. Twenty-five windows are located in the crown. Lady Liberty's torch was open to the public until 1916. It closed after a bomb exploded during World War I. No one has been in the torch since.

212-363-3200
nps.gov/stli

ROAD TRIP TRIVIA QUESTION #70
What is inscribed on the Statue of Liberty's tablet,
and what do her seven crowns represent?

THE WHITE HOUSE

It's not only the private residence of the president of the United States but also the most recognized house in the entire world. In recent years, getting close to the White House has become more difficult with security fears. Still, you can easily take a photo of the north side of the mansion just beyond the new, higher fence. Of course, you never know what antics you'll witness when you visit. Protesters, people from all over the world, and a handful of interesting characters are always sure to be in the mix.

To take a free White House tour, you'll need to contact the office of a senator from your state. Plan early, as space is extremely limited. For just a quick look and to pose for an outdoor photo, use the McPherson Square stop on the DC Metro train for quickest access.

1600 Pennsylvania Ave.
Washington, DC 20500
whitehouse.gov

ROAD TRIP TRIVIA QUESTION #71
What world leader refused to ever again stay in the Lincoln Bedroom after Lincoln's ghost appeared to him beside the fireplace as he was emerging from a bath, fully nude?

REGULAR

THIS SALE

$ □.□□

GALLON AND SALE INDICATIONS MUST BE AT ZERO
WHEN DELIVERY IS BEGUN — UNDER PENALTY OF LAW

GALLONS

□ □ □ ¢

PER GALLON
ALL TAXES INCLUDED

ACCURATE DELIVERY FROM 3 GAL. PER MIN. TO FULL FLOW AT ANY PRESSURE

ROAD TRIPS

EXPLORE THE
MISSISSIPPI BLUES TRAIL

Nearly all modern-day music can be traced back to the plantations of Mississippi where the Blues was born in the nineteenth century. The lyrics were more than just cries of despair or adversity. These songs became vessels to channel raw emotions—good and bad. The Mississippi Blues Trail is a collection of important people and places that helped shape the full story of the genre, from the birthplace of Muddy Waters to the spot in Tutwiler, Mississippi, where W. C. Handy first encountered a man playing slide guitar with a knife.

Besides historical spots, such as the 100 Men Hall in Bay Saint Louis or the childhood home of Elvis in Tupelo, consider visiting some of the many Blues museums in the state. The Gateway to the Blues Museum off Highway 61 in Tunica is the perfect starting place for tourists who know everything—or nothing—about the Blues.

msbluestrail.org

ROAD TRIP TRIVIA QUESTION #72
What legendary Blues musician is believed to have sold his soul in exchange for his brilliant guitar-playing skills?

Gateway to the Blues Museum

13625 Hwy. 61
N., Tunica Resorts, MS 38664
888-488-6422
tunicatravel.com/blues

Elvis Presley Birthplace & Museum

306 Elvis Presley Dr.
Tupelo, MS 38801
662-841-1245
elvispresleybirthplace.com

100 Men Hall

303 Union St.
Bay St. Louis, MS 39520
100menhall.org

The BB King Museum

400 Second St.
Indianola, MS 38751
662-887-9539
bbkingmuseum.org

Delta Blues Museum

Blues Alley Ln.
Clarksdale, MS 38614
662-627-6820

GET YOUR KICKS ON ROUTE 66

America's most well-known highway earned its legacy status by serving as a westward path for motorists during the Dust Bowl era of the 1930s. Often called the "Mother Road" or "Main Street of America," Route 66 stretched 2,448 miles across eight states, from Chicago, Illinois, to Santa Monica, California. While it was officially declassified in 1985, travelers from around the world still crave the Americana of themed motels and quirky roadside attractions that still exist today. Large sections of the original highway are still easily accessible, but be prepared to take plenty of detours if you plan to be a Route 66 purist.

Hundreds of books, websites, and groups are devoted to preserving the old highway's legacy and inspiring another generation of travelers to get their kicks!

historic66.com
theroute-66.com
national66.org
drivingroute66.com
route66guide.com

ROAD TRIP TRIVIA QUESTION #73

What 2006 Pixar film was inspired by a family road trip on historic Route 66?

TRAVEL ON THE
BEARTOOTH SCENIC BYWAY
INTO YELLOWSTONE NATIONAL PARK

It's been called the most scenic drive in America. It took all of about five minutes before I understood why and completely agreed. I was fortunate enough to drive this sixty-eight-mile highway with my dad in the summer of 2016. At nearly every twist and turn, we both were amazed at the majestic views through Montana and Wyoming. I don't think it's a stretch to add that at times it almost felt as though we were on another planet, with landscapes I've never witnessed.

Your best bet is starting in Red Lodge, Montana, and traveling west on US Highway 212 until you reach the northern entrance of Yellowstone National Park. If you plan to explore the highway in only one day, give yourself plenty of time, as you will stop many times to soak in the views. The highway is open from around Memorial Day until October, depending on snowfall. Be sure to check weather conditions, as it's also been called one of the most dangerous highways in America.

beartoothhighway.com

ROAD TRIP TRIVIA QUESTION #74
What legendary CBS travel journalist called the Beartooth Scenic Byway "the greatest drive in America"?

TAKE A RIDE ALONG NEWFOUND GAP ROAD
IN THE SMOKY MOUNTAINS

This popular road is situated in the middle of the Great Smoky Mountains National Park between North Carolina and Tennessee. Its most popular spots include the Rockefeller Memorial, where President Franklin D. Roosevelt dedicated the national park in 1940. The thirty-one-mile road is open all year long and stretches from the Sugarlands Visitor Center in Gatlinburg all the way to Cherokee, North Carolina. It is the only paved stretch of road of America's most visited national park.

Newfound Gap Road provides some of the best views of the park but also leads to the turnoff for the highest point in the Smoky Mountains—Clingman's Dome. Be sure to bring a jacket, even in the summer months, as temperatures can be much cooler at the higher elevations. Smoky Mountains National Park does not charge an admission fee.

Sugarlands Visitor Center
1420 Fighting Creek Gap Rd.
Gatlinburg, TN 37738
865-436-1200

Clingman's Dome Visitor Center
Clingmans Dome Rd.
Bryson City, NC 28713
865-436-1200

ROAD TRIP TRIVIA QUESTION #75
The Smoky Mountains are known as the "salamander capital of the world." How do these amphibians breathe?

EXPERIENCE TRAIL RIDGE ROAD
IN ROCKY MOUNTAIN NATIONAL PARK

The most popular route through Rocky Mountain National Park has more than lived up to expectations set by the National Park Service back in 1931. The forty-eight-mile long Trail Ridge Road is the highest continuous paved road in the country. It showcases a wide variety of majestic scenery from top to bottom. From hundreds of plant species to bighorn sheep and pikas, you'll witness an abundance of memorable views. You'll even cross the Continental Divide at one point on your journey. At night, you can see the city lights of Denver and even Fort Collins from Rainbow Curve.

Begin the drive in Estes Park after a stop at the historic Stanley Hotel (the setting for Stephen King's *The Shining*) and wind up at elevations over 12,000 feet. Eleven miles of the road is above the treeline. Because of snowfall, the road is only open from late May until October. You should plan to spend at least half the day exploring!

Alpine Visitor Center
Trail Ridge Rd.
Grand Lake, CO 80447
970-586-1222
rockymountainnationalpark.com

ROAD TRIP TRIVIA QUESTION #76
Because of their distinct presence in the state of Colorado, what animal is the symbol for Colorado Parks & Wildlife and Rocky Mountain National Park?

DRIVE WITH THE TOP DOWN
ON PACIFIC COAST HIGHWAY

Starting in the forests of western Washington and heading south 1,650 miles to the Mexican border, the PCH has enough remarkable places to stop for an entire series of travel books. You'll drive along the peaceful Oregon coastline and see quaint towns and statuesque lighthouses. In California, see its magnificent redwoods, seaside villages, wineries, boardwalks, beaches, and maybe a movie star.

A few big stops along the way include Olympic National Park, Portland, San Francisco, the Santa Cruz Beach Boardwalk, Big Sur, Malibu, Long Beach, Los Angeles, and San Diego. In total, it will take you about ten days to drive the entire route, but for the best road trip experience, plan on two weeks to soak in all the beauty and fun experiences along the way. Traveling in the off season (not July or August) will enhance your trip. One often overlooked idea is to drive one way and catch the Amtrak Coast Starlight train back to Los Angeles or Seattle.

ROAD TRIP TRIVIA QUESTION #77

What is the name of the famous ship that's docked in Long Beach, California? It was called the Grey Ghost during World War II and was quite important to the Allied Powers.

FUN STOPS ALONG THE WAY

Monterey Aquarium
Located on the ocean's edge, it's one of the
best aquariums in the world.

886 Cannery Row
Monterey, CA 93940
831-648-4800

Chandelier Tree
A giant redwood tree that you can drive through
(for a small fee). Your large SUV might not fit.
But traveling in a smaller vehicle? Go for it.

67402 Drive Thru Tree Rd.
Leggett, CA 95585
707-925-6464

Santa Cruz Beach Boardwalk
Hop on the Giant Dipper, a wooden coaster that
opened in 1924. Enjoy thrift stores, paddleboarding,
and views of sea lions and sailboats.

400 Beach St.
Santa Cruz, CA 95060
831-423-5590

Oregon Lighthouses
Seven of the eleven lighthouses on the Oregon
coast are open to the public.

visittheoregoncoast.com/lighthouses

Coronado Beach
Shopping, dining, golf, and recreation in
beautiful weather year-round.

coronadovisitorcenter.com

TAKE NEWPORT'S FAMOUS TEN MILE DRIVE

Rhode Island's most popular drive transports you back to the 1800s when wealthy New Yorkers spent their summers in gigantic cottages with beautiful ocean views. Cruisin' around the ten-mile loop, the Atlantic Ocean is on one side, while beautiful estates fill up the view through your other car window. Take some time to enjoy the breeze off the water while sitting on a park bench, or perhaps enjoy a picnic at Fort Adams State Park. Taylor Swift, Conan O'Brien, and Debra Messing reportedly own homes along the road.

You can tour a handful of historic estates, visit the International Tennis Hall of Fame, and see St. Mary's Church, where John F. Kennedy and Jacqueline Bouvier were married. In warmer months, find a spot along the way to catch some sun or work on your tan. Just be careful before taking a dip in the water. It's probably pretty chilly unless it's August.

oceandrivenewport.com
visitrhodeisland.com

ROAD TRIP TRIVIA QUESTION #78
What celebrity and voice actor was raised in Rhode Island, which inspired many of the scenes and characters in his hit television series?

RIDE ALONG THE OVERSEAS HIGHWAY

A whopping 113 miles of roadway, including forty-two bridges, make up one of the most unique drives in all of America. You'll start in Miami and head to Key West on US Route 1 to soak in tropical views, including water in all shades of green and blue. Sometimes referred to as the "magic carpet," the Overseas Highway provides a route through the biggest area of coral reefs on the US mainland. The Seven Mile Bridge is among the highlights of the journey, especially if timed at sunrise or sunset.

The trail began in 1912 as a railroad line but was destroyed in a 1935 hurricane. The rails were later converted to highways. This is one part of the country where road rage doesn't seem to exist too often. Being stuck in traffic means extra time to drink in the gorgeous ocean views.

fla-keys.com/the-highway-that-goes-to-sea

ROAD TRIP TRIVIA QUESTION #79

The iconic Seven Mile Bridge has been used in various films and TV series over the years. What 1994 American spy movie starring Jamie Lee Curtis featured a scene on the bridge?

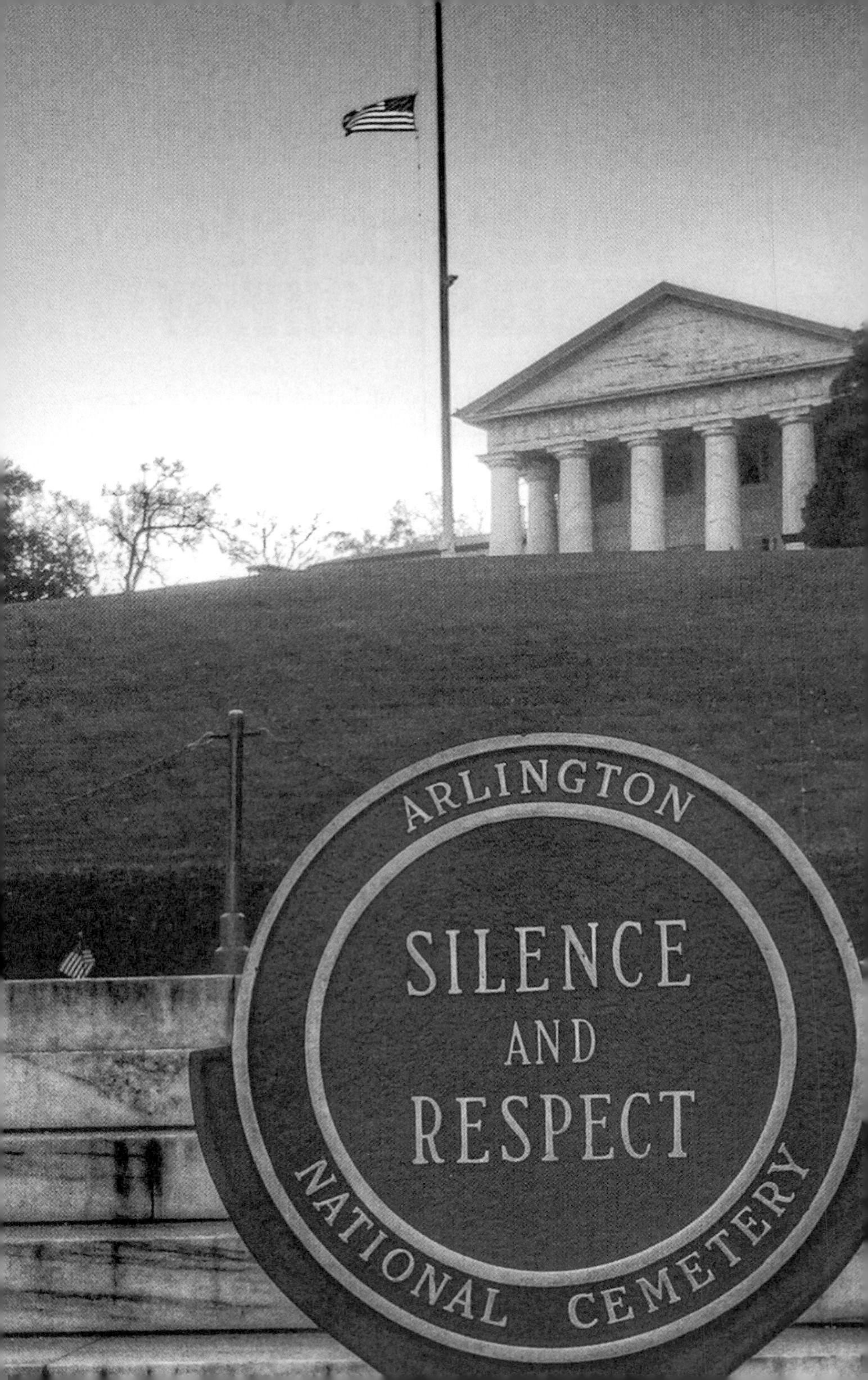
ARLINGTON
SILENCE
AND
RESPECT
NATIONAL CEMETERY

AMERICAN HISTORY AND CULTURE

VISIT ABRAHAM LINCOLN'S HOME
AND USE THE HANDRAIL

The only home Abraham Lincoln ever owned is located in Springfield, Illinois. For seventeen years, the Lincoln family lived in the neighborhood now run by the National Park Service. His two-story, twelve-room home and the four blocks around it can be toured for free. Today, the home consists of replicated furniture and décor that would have been found inside in the mid-1800s.

Two things are still inside the home that are original to when Lincoln lived in Springfield—a small desk upstairs and the handrail on the stairs between the first and second floors. You can touch that same handrail the future president used on a daily basis. Also be sure to visit the old state capitol downtown, Lincoln's law office, his final resting place, and the incredible Abraham Lincoln Presidential Library & Museum.

413 S. Eighth St.
Springfield, IL 62701
217-492-4241
nps.gov/liho

ROAD TRIP TRIVIA QUESTION #80
Which of the following are true statements about Abraham Lincoln? He never slept in the Lincoln Bedroom. He was a licensed bartender. He is in the Wrestling Hall of Fame.

IN THE NEIGHBORHOOD

Abraham Lincoln Presidential Library & Museum

112 N. Sixth St.
Springfield, IL 62701
217-558-8844
alplm.org

Lincoln-Herndon Law Offices

Sixth & Adams Sts.
Springfield, IL 62701
217-785-7289

Lincoln Tomb & Monument

1500 Monument Ave.
Springfield, IL 62702
217-782-2717

Springfield State Capitol Building

ilstatehouse.com

The Lincoln Depot

lincolndepot.org

SEE THE CHARTERS OF FREEDOM

The documents most instrumental in the founding of America can be located inside the National Archives building in Washington, DC. Commonly referred to as the "Charters of Freedom," the Declaration of Independence, the Constitution, and the Bill of Rights are all available for public viewing inside a well-guarded rotunda inside the building. The three documents are behind bulletproof glass in bronze cases under low lights and cool room temperatures. This is their most recent home, where they have been on display since 1953. Before then the Library of Congress and even Fort Knox stored them.

After seeing these historic documents, you can visit the many other exhibits in the Archives that feature everything from presidential speeches to the arrest warrant for Lee Harvey Oswald. The National Archives and Records Administration (NARA) is the nation's official recordkeeper, saving the most important documents pertaining to the business of the federal government.

700 Pennsylvania Ave. NW
Washington, DC 20408
archives.gov

ROAD TRIP TRIVIA QUESTION #81
Of all the records stored within the National Archives system, which government agency has the most amount of material stored?

TALK WITH A VETERAN
AT THE NATIONAL WWII MUSEUM

New Orleans is known for a lot of things, but its biggest attraction may surprise you. The National WWII Museum is one of the finest museums I have ever visited (and I've been to a lot of them!). The entire complex of galleries and exhibits tells the story of the global conflict in ways that are easy to understand and compelling. There are interactive experiences, such as working on board a submarine, and a 4D film that perfectly sums up World War II in a presentation that is simply outstanding. You'll need more than one day to see everything on display.

The best part of visiting the museum is getting a chance to mingle with military veterans, in particular those who served in World War II. You'd be well served to talk with them, listen to their stories, and thank them personally for helping to save the world.

945 Magazine St.
New Orleans, LA 70130
504-528-1944
nationalww2museum.org

ROAD TRIP TRIVIA QUESTION #82
Why is the National WWII Museum located in New Orleans?

VISIT THE ALAMO

Thousands of Mexican forces stormed the Alamo in February 1836 as around two hundred brave defenders held on for thirteen days. Though the battle was lost, the site has remained a sacred reminder of independence and freedom—something Texans in particular take quite seriously. You could call it a rallying moment for Texans, as the Alamo battle inspired another fight, this time in San Jacinto, directly leading to Texas independence. In a bizarre historical twist, it turned out that the Alamo was actually ordered to be destroyed by General Sam Houston shortly before the Mexicans launched their offense on it.

Admission is free. For a small fee, you can take guided tours of the entire site. Be sure to check out the exhibit of priceless artifacts donated by musician Phil Collins. The collection contains weapons, relics, and original documents.

300 Alamo Plaza
San Antonio, TX 78205
210-225-1391
thealamo.org

ROAD TRIP TRIVIA QUESTION #83
This iconic American statesman ran away from home at the age of thirteen, became a congressman, and eventually died during the battle of the Alamo. What was his name?

WALK THROUGH THE BAGGAGE ROOM
AT ELLIS ISLAND

The baggage room of Ellis Island may be a place most tourists quickly pass through. Standing near the exhibit of centuries-old suitcases and heavy trunks, try to imagine the mass chaos that took place here as millions of immigrants came through Ellis Island. Those who couldn't afford a first-class or second-class boat ticket had to pass through here, facing mental and medical tests before being granted citizenship. They were brave and determined men, women, and children who left their homelands for a chance of experiencing "the American dream." Many arrived with nothing more than a suitcase and high hopes for opportunity.

The baggage room was commonly referred to as a "logistical nightmare," with thousands of immigrants checking bags every day. Today, the room serves as the entrance to the Ellis Island Immigration Museum, where visitors can trace the steps of their ancestors who started their new life in the United States.

212-363-3200
nps.gov/elis

ROAD TRIP TRIVIA QUESTION #84
Immigrants who could afford a first-class or second-class ticket on the steamboats coming to America were inspected and allowed to enter the US with little fanfare. Ellis Island processed the immigrants who could only afford the third and least expensive onboard accommodations. What did they call this dirty, crowded portion of the ship?

GO TO HUFFMAN PRAIRIE FIELD AND LOOK UP

This stop requires a bit of imagination, but it's definitely an important place in American history. Huffman Prairie Field is where the Wright Brothers mastered the art of flying. It's hard to imagine a world without airplanes, and it was in this open field (or above it) that the marvel of flight took shape. Natives of Dayton, Ohio, Wilbur and Orville Wright used the land that now sits next to Wright-Patterson Air Force Base to design the world's first "practical airplane."

The Wright Flyer II made its first turn and circle in the air above the field here in 1904. In that first year, there were 105 flights totaling forty-five minutes in the air. By 1910, Huffman Prairie Field was used for a flying school. The Wright Brothers would use the property until 1916. Besides the field, be sure to visit the other Wright Brothers historic sites in Dayton.

Pylon Rd.
Wright-Patterson AFB, OH 45433
937-425-0008
nps.gov/daav

ROAD TRIP TRIVIA QUESTION #85
In 1906, what was the Wright Brothers' first invention labeled as on the actual patent?

IN THE NEIGHBORHOOD

Huffman Prairie Flying Field Interpretive Center

Wright-Patterson Air Force Base
2380 Memorial Rd.
Dayton, OH 45402
937-425-0008

Wright-Dunbar Interpretive Center

16 S. Williams St.
Dayton, OH 45402
937-225-7705

Hawthorn Hill

901 Harman Ave.
Dayton, OH 45419
937-293-2841

Carillon Historical Park

1000 Carillon Blvd.
Dayton, OH 45409
937-293-2841
daytonhistory.org

National Museum of the US Air Force

1100 Spaatz St.
Dayton, OH 45431
937-255-3286
www.nationalmuseum.af.mil

EXPLORE THE FREEDOM TRAIL

Boston is full of historic sites that tell the story of America's formative years. The Freedom Trail is a two and a half mile long path that takes tourists to sixteen different historically significant places. You'll find the Old State House where the Declaration of Independence was first read aloud and a statue of Ben Franklin where he attended the Boston Latin School. Other stops along the Freedom Trail include the site of the Boston Massacre, the Paul Revere House, and Bunker Hill Monument.

One of the most awesome things to see while walking the trail is the USS *Constitution*. Launched in 1797, it's America's oldest commissioned warship. It was sometimes referred to as "Old Ironsides" because cannonballs appeared to bounce off the side of the ship when it was under attack. A museum with hands-on exhibits relating to the battleship is just steps away. It is free to walk the trail, but some sites do charge an entrance fee.

139 Tremont St.
Boston, MA 02111
617-357-8300
thefreedomtrail.org

ROAD TRIP TRIVIA QUESTION #86
The oldest public park in America is located along the Freedom Trail. What is it called?

VISIT A PRESIDENTIAL LIBRARY

No matter what your political leanings may be, each presidential library & museum is a priceless time capsule into American life under each president. You'll see such things as Truman's "The Buck Stops Here" sign, the first Oval Office telephone, Eisenhower's traveling podium, and Jimmy Carter's Grammy award. The megaphone used by George W. Bush after the September 11, 2001, terrorist attacks and the tools used in the Watergate break-in are also on display.

Most of the museums include an Oval Office replica and displays of gifts given to each president from world leaders. Some of the most interesting artifacts are once "top secret" documents and, of course, campaign materials, such as buttons and yard signs. Visiting all these institutions will be the most rewarding American history lesson you can give to your children (or yourself!).

archives.gov/presidential-libraries

ROAD TRIP TRIVIA QUESTION #87

Can you name the state that has the most presidential libraries and which presidents they belong to?

George W. Bush Presidential Library and Museum

2943 SMU Blvd.
Dallas, TX 75205
214-346-1557

William J. Clinton Presidential Library & Museum

1200 Clinton Ave.
Little Rock, AR 72201
501-374-4242

George H. W. Bush Library & Museum

1000 George Bush Dr.
West College Station, TX 77845
979-691-4000

Ronald Reagan Presidential Library and Museum

40 Presidential Dr.
Simi Valley, CA 93065
805-522-2977

Jimmy Carter Library & Museum

441 Freedom Pkwy.
Atlanta, GA 30307
404-865-7100

Gerald R. Ford Presidential Museum

1000 Beal Ave.
Ann Arbor, MI 48109
734-205-0555

Richard Nixon Presidential Library & Museum

18001 Yorba Linda Blvd.
Yorba Linda, CA 92886
714-983-9120

Lyndon B. Johnson Library & Museum

2313 Red River St.
Austin, TX 78705
512-721-0200

John F. Kennedy Presidential Library & Museum

Columbia Point
Boston, MA 02125
866-JFK-1960

Dwight D. Eisenhower Presidential Library & Museum

200 SE Fourth St.
Abilene, KS 67410
785-263-6700

Harry S. Truman Library & Museum

500 W. US Highway 24
Independence, MO 64050-1798
816-833-1225

Franklin D. Roosevelt Presidential Library and Museum

4079 Albany Post Rd.
Hyde Park, NY 12538
845-486-7770

Herbert Hoover Presidential Library & Museum

210 Parkside Dr.
West Branch, IA 52358
319-643-5301

Abraham Lincoln Presidential Library & Museum

212 N. Sixth St.
Springfield, IL 62701
217-753-4900

TOUR THE USS ALABAMA

Standing on board the deck of this massive ship quickly reminds you of the power and ingenuity of the United States military. From stem to stern, the warship is a whopping 680 feet long. Now permanently docked in Mobile, the USS *Alabama* first saw battle shortly after the Japanese attacks on Pearl Harbor. The ship eventually led the fleet into Tokyo Bay for the signing of the formal surrender documents during World War II.

By 1964, the Navy decided to scrap the USS *Alabama*, but local school children raised money to save it. They raised $100,000 in small change as part of a fund-raising effort to help place the ship on display and preserve it for future generations. Three self-guided tours are available. Bring comfortable closed-toe shoes, as you'll be doing a lot of walking as well as climbing up and down ladders and stairs.

2703 Battleship Pkwy.
Mobile, AL 36603
251-433-2703
ussalabama.com

ROAD TRIP TRIVIA QUESTION #88
The USS *Alabama* portrayed the USS *Missouri* in what 1992 action film?

TOUCH A WITNESS TREE
IN GETTYSBURG

You'll feel a bizarre range of emotions while standing on the battlefields of Gettysburg, Pennsylvania. On one hand, especially on a clear day, the scenery is absolutely beautiful. On the other hand, you feel a sense of guilt for enjoying its beauty where so many people fought and died on the very same spot where you're standing.

Many noteworthy monuments and statues are located in Gettysburg, but seeing a tree that actually witnessed the battle will truly take your breath away. Only about a hundred "Witness Trees" are left, with more dying annually from weather or disease. Many have bullets still inside their trunks. The visitor center offers a great vehicle tour, where a licensed battlefield guide will drive your car and narrate while you and your family are free to sit back and look out the windows without distractions. The guide will be able to point out the trees during your tour.

1195 Baltimore Pike
Gettysburg, PA 17325
717-338-1243
gettysburgfoundation.org

ROAD TRIP TRIVIA QUESTION #89
Gettysburg is best known for its history and role in the Civil War, but it's also home to a fun, quirky museum that holds more than 12,000 dolls, toys, and figurines of what animal?

SING THE NATIONAL ANTHEM AT
FORT McHENRY

Best known as the place that inspired America's national anthem, Fort McHenry is a treasured historic site in Baltimore, Maryland. Francis Scott Key penned a poem called "Defence of Fort McHenry" after seeing the American flag still flying at the fort following twenty-five hours of British bombing. The words of his poem were set to music and became a patriotic song called "The Star-Spangled Banner." In 1931 it became the national anthem of the United States.

Visitors can take a guided or self-guided tour of the fort and enjoy the on-site museum. On a nice day, it's a perfect spot to enjoy a picnic lunch. The grounds also have paths for bikes and walking. Fall and winter have the fewest crowds, but brace yourself for the cold air that whisks in off the bay! No matter the season, the views are fantastic.

2400 E. Fort Ave.
Baltimore, MD 21230
410-962-4290

ROAD TRIP TRIVIA QUESTION #90
How many stars and stripes were on the flag flying at Fort McHenry when Francis Scott Key penned what became "The Star-Spangled Banner"?

IN THE NEIGHBORHOOD

National Aquarium

501 E. Pratt St.
Baltimore, MD 21202
410-576-3800
aqua.org

Babe Ruth Birthplace

216 Emory St.
Baltimore, MD 21230
baberuthmuseum.org

National Museum of Dentistry

31 S. Greene St.
Baltimore, MD 21201
410-706-0600
dentalmuseum.org

Edgar Allan Poe Grave

515 W. Fayette St.
Baltimore, MD 21201
410-706-2072

Oriole Park at Camden Yards

333 W. Camden St.
Baltimore, MD 21202
baltimore.orioles.mlb.com

GRAND OLE OPRY:
STAND IN THE CENTER CIRCLE

First broadcasting in 1925, the Opry remains the world's longest running radio show. Each week country music still fills the airwaves from the stage's sacred circle in Nashville, Tennessee. Originally known as the WSM Barn Dance, growing audiences forced the country music program to eventually land at the Ryman Auditorium downtown in 1943. In 1974 the Grand Ole Opry House became the show's permanent home. The 4,000-seat auditorium is full each week, as guests witness new country music artists performing with longtime Opry performers.

The circle at center stage was cut from the floor at the Ryman Auditorium. It's a significant moment for musicians knowing that so many legends have stood there. Elvis, Patsy Cline, Hank Williams, and the current superstars of the genre have all stood on the same wood flooring. Today, a backstage tour allows visitors the chance to stand there as well.

2804 Opryland Dr.
Nashville, TN 37214
1-800-SEE-OPRY
opry.com

ROAD TRIP TRIVIA QUESTION #91
What president played piano on the Opry stage when its current home opened to the public?

IN THE NEIGHBORHOOD

Country Music Hall of Fame

222 Fifth Ave.
Nashville, TN 37203
615-416-2001
countrymusichalloffame.org

Ryman Auditorium

116 Fifth Ave.
Nashville, TN 37203
615-889-3060
ryman.com

Lane Motor Museum

702 Murfreesboro Pike
Nashville, TN 37210
615-742-7445
lanemotormuseum.org

George Jones Museum

128 Second Ave.
Nashville, TN 37201
615-818-0128
georgejones.com

Goo Goo Clusters Shop

116 Third Ave.
Nashville, TN 37201
615-490-6685
googoo.com

PAY YOUR RESPECTS AT PEARL HARBOR

This is the only item on this list that obviously can't be part of a road trip, but it's important enough to include in the book. FDR correctly said it was a "date which will live in infamy," referring to December 7, 1941, when Japan attacked the US military base at Pearl Harbor. Today, visitors can experience four different historic sites on the Hawaiian island of Oahu that tell the story of that tragic day in America's history.

It will take you at least an entire day to visit all four sites. They include the USS *Arizona* Memorial, Battleship *Missouri* Memorial, USS *Bowfin* Submarine Museum and Park, and Pacific Aviation Museum. Tickets for each site can be purchased online before your visit. Pearl Harbor is still an active military base and headquarters of the US Navy Pacific Fleet.

pearlharborhistoricsites.org
ussmissouri.org
bowfin.org
pacificaviationmuseum.org

ROAD TRIP TRIVIA QUESTION #92

The Battleship Missouri was the last American battleship ever built and the last to be decommissioned. The surrender of the Japanese on the deck of the Missouri brought the Second World War to an end. What was the battleship's nickname?

VISIT INDEPENDENCE HALL

If you're looking for a spot that truly marks where America began, this is the place. The rooms in this building gave birth to the greatest experiment in the history of nations. The idea of self-governing and a system of checks and balances for those in power started at Independence Hall. It's considered "the birthplace of America," as the Declaration of Independence and US Constitution were both signed here in the building's Assembly Room. While touring Independence Hall, you'll see where George Washington was appointed commander in chief of the Continental Army, the Articles of Confederation were adopted, and the Constitutional Convention took place. Following his assassination, Abraham Lincoln's body lay in repose here for two days.

No fees are charged to visit Independence Hall, although a ticket from the National Park Service is required. Visitors can also see the Liberty Bell, which is within a short walking distance.

143 S. Third St.
Philadelphia, PA 19106
212-965-2305
nps.gov/inde

ROAD TRIP TRIVIA QUESTION #93

The first inscription on the Liberty Bell is a Bible verse:
"Proclaim liberty throughout all the land unto all inhabitants thereof."
What book of the Bible is it from?

SIT ON THE BUS SEAT
THAT ROSA PARKS REFUSED TO GIVE UP

Inside the Henry Ford Museum in Dearborn, Michigan, sits the very bus where civil rights icon Rosa Parks made a stand for equality on December 1, 1955. In fact, she did so by not standing at all. As her bus in Montgomery, Alabama, was filling up with white passengers, she was asked to move. She refused to give up her seat and was arrested. She'd later say that she was "tired of giving in" when asked why she decided not to give up her seat.

After experiencing some time in the historic bus, be prepared to spend an entire day at the Henry Ford Museum. Some of the more interesting items on display include the Oscar-Mayer Wiener mobile, the Wright Brothers' first bike shop, and Thomas Edison's laboratory. The museum also includes two artifacts related to presidential assassinations: the chair in which Lincoln was shot and JFK's limo.

20900 Oakwood Blvd.
Dearborn, MI 48124
313-982-6001
thehenryford.org

ROAD TRIP TRIVIA QUESTION #94
Where was Rosa Parks sitting on the bus?

SEPTEMBER 11 MEMORIAL

The terrorist attacks on September 11, 2001, forever changed the United States of America. On a clear fall morning in New York City, two hijacked airplanes slammed into the World Trade Center, killing thousands and sending shock waves through the world. It was the largest loss of life from a foreign attack on American soil in our country's history.

The National September 11 Memorial and Museum is located where the World Trade Center once stood. Its reflecting pools are each nearly an acre in size and feature the largest man-made waterfalls in North America. The names of every person who died in the 2001 and 1993 attacks are inscribed into bronze panels. The memorial also pays tribute to the people who died in separate attacks at the Pentagon and near Shanksville, Pennsylvania.

180 Greenwich St.
New York, NY 10007
212-312-8800
911memorial.org

ROAD TRIP TRIVIA QUESTION #95
As a result of the terrorist attacks,
what new US government agency was formed?

WATCH A CASE
AT THE US SUPREME COURT

Did you know that the general public can watch cases at the US Supreme Court? The nation's highest court allows visitors the opportunity to watch history in the making as justices hear oral arguments. From Brown v. Board of Education to Bush v. Gore, the court's decisions can shape a generation of American laws and culture. To experience a Supreme Court case, you'll need to show up early and stand in line. Court police will escort those in line to the courtroom, where you are allowed to watch for three minutes before moving on so that others have a chance to watch the proceedings. You can check the court's website for a calendar of when the court is in session.

On most days, an informative lecture is available inside the courtroom, where visitors will learn all the rules, traditions, and procedures that take place inside the US Supreme Court. No photographs are allowed inside the courtroom.

1 First St. NE
Washington, DC 20543
supremecourt.gov

ROAD TRIP TRIVIA QUESTION #96
How many Supreme Court justices were confirmed under President Obama?

STAND IN SILENCE
AT ARLINGTON NATIONAL CEMETERY

The remains of more than 400,000 people from the US and eleven other countries are buried here in Arlington, Virginia. Nearly five thousand of those are unidentified or "unknown soldiers." The cemetery is the second largest in the country, with more than four million visitors annually. Flags at Arlington National Cemetery are flown at half-staff from a half hour before the first funeral until a half hour after the last funeral each day.

Active, retired, and former members of the armed forces, Medal of Honor recipients, high-ranking federal government officials, and their dependents can be buried at Arlington. John F. Kennedy and Howard Taft are the only presidents buried on the grounds. Standing among the thousands of tombstones is an overwhelming emotional experience for most. Volunteers place US flags at each gravesite for the Memorial Day holiday, making it among the best times to visit.

877-907-8585
www.arlingtoncemetery.mil

ROAD TRIP TRIVIA QUESTION #97
The soldiers from which four US wars are memorialized at the Tomb of the Unknowns in Arlington National Cemetery?

CLIMB INSIDE A GIANT TRACTOR AT
THE JOHN DEERE PAVILION

It's hard to imagine driving past any farmland in America without spotting those iconic green and yellow John Deere tractors. Now a global company, John Deere revolutionized the way America's farmers tended their crops and helped keep our families fed. His invention of the self-scouring steel plow helped develop the Midwest United States. By 1923, Deere & Company was mass-producing tractors. The model "D" was its first commercial success and continued being sold until 1953.

Inside the John Deere Pavilion, you'll see the latest of these incredible machines up close and even have the opportunity to climb inside. While you're in the Quad Cities region, plan to experience all the different sites related to John Deere. You can visit his home and blacksmith shop, explore a tractor and engine museum, and even tour the John Deere Factory and world headquarters.

1400 River Dr.
Moline, IL 61265
309-765-1000
deere.com

ROAD TRIP TRIVIA QUESTION #98
True or false: John Deere, the most famous name in tractors, never actually saw one in person.

VISIT OCMULGEE NATIONAL MONUMENT

You could call it a hidden gem of Macon, Georgia. The Ocmulgee National Monument includes a Native American earth lodge with its original floor. Scientists have determined that it dates all the way back to 1015. You will have to duck your head while stepping through the door. Once inside, you'll witness exactly what it looked like when the original inhabitants used it as a formal council chamber. You'll also notice the only known example of a spiral mound in North America. It's twenty feet high and was used from around 1350 to the late 1500s.

Two Clovis spear points have been uncovered at Ocmulgee. These were tools used by humans to attack animals. It's noteworthy because these tools are the oldest evidence of humans in the United States.

1207 Emery Highway
Macon, GA 31217
478-752-8257 x222
nps.gov/ocmu

ROAD TRIP TRIVIA QUESTION #99

Another popular tourist attraction in Macon, Georgia, is called "The Big House." It's the former home of what popular 1970s band?
HINT: The lyrics to one of its most popular songs mention "rolling down Highway 41," which runs right in front of the house.

TAKE A TOUR OF HARVARD UNIVERSITY

Established in 1636, Harvard is the oldest institution of higher learning in the United States. The Harvard Library is the largest academic library in the world. Its museum holds more than twenty-eight million works of art. The campus offers tours led by students, and the grounds are perfect for photographers looking to capture shots of great Early American architecture.

The John Harvard statue in front of University Hall is one of the most photographed statues in the United States. Tradition is to touch the left foot and you will magically gain some of the knowledge of Harvard University. (Note: Some students participate in a different "tradition" that may lead you to avoid touching that foot at all!) Tours begin at the Office of Admissions.

617-495-1551
college.harvard.edu/admissions/visit

ROAD TRIP TRIVIA QUESTION #100

How many Harvard students went on to become US presidents?
Bonus points if you can name all of them!

TRIVIA ANSWERS

1. There was a ban on fireworks.
2. 1956
3. Passion Pits
4. 1963
5. *Mrs. Doubtfire*
6. "Deep in the Heart of Texas"
7. Pizza Hut (1958)
8. 1906 San Francisco Earthquake
9. Five cents
10. Barack Obama
11. It took ten people.
12. AK, DE, HI, ID, ME, MT, NH, ND, RI, SD, and VT
13. "I Got You Babe" (Sonny and Cher)
14. Oregon
15. The cords were made to screw into a light socket.
16. Thirty-two (sixteen on each side)
17. Atlanta
18. Bill Clinton on October 25, 1998
19. Microsoft, Amazon, Costco, and Starbucks
20. Fourth grade
21. Twenty two thousand
22. Mashed potato or laundry soap flakes
23. Alan Freed

24. The original board was in the shape of a circle like most dining room tables at the time.

25. Elvis Presley

26. Golden Driller

27. *Million Dollar Quartet*

28. Seattle, WA

29. False—they have no vocal cords

30. Bagels

31. Jefferson City, MO; Madison, WI; and Lincoln, NE

32. Gateway Arch in Saint Louis

33. Mexican food

34. Frank Sinatra

35. Dolly Parton

36. Fourth of July

37. Eight (four walking legs, four swimming legs)

38. Three

39. Thomas Jefferson

40. Cheese dip (Little Rock even hosts the World Cheese Dip Championships!)

41. *A League of Their Own*

42. All of these at the same time would fit inside the track's oval.

43. Trees with flowers or shrubs

44. Wrigley Field (1914) and Dodger Stadium (1962)

45. Red

46. "Bang the Drum All Day" by Todd Rundgren

47. Illinois

48. *Leatherheads*

49. Men

50. Colorado (eastern half) and Mojave (western half)

51. Little Missouri River

52. The Natural State

53. True.

54. Morgantown

55. It's the only place on Earth where both of these animals coexist.

56. Germany (thirty-six); USA was second (thirty-four)

57. About seventy percent of the Louisville Zoo

58. Zero

59. Los Angeles hosted the Olympics.

60. The "unsinkable" Molly Brown

61. Peachtree

62. Nelson-Atkins Museum of Art (Rozzelle Court Fountain)

63. Howard Hughes

64. One hundred and twenty miles

65. John Wayne

66. Red stick

67. Dickies

68. Superior, Michigan, Huron, and Erie

69. *Vegas Vacation*

70. July 4, 1776, and the seven oceans and continents

71. Winston Churchill

72. Robert Johnson

73. *Cars*

74. Charles Kuralt

75. They breathe through their skin.

76. Bighorn sheep

77. Queen Mary

78. Seth MacFarlane (*Family Guy*)

79. *True Lies*

80. All three are true!

81. NASA

82. It's where the Higgins boats were produced during WWII.

83. Davy Crockett

84. Steerage

85. "Flying Machine"

86. Boston Common

87. Texas (Johnson and both Bush presidents)

88. *Under Siege*

89. The Elephant—At Mr. Ed's Elephant Museum

90. Fifteen—It was the only US flag to have more than thirteen stripes

91. Richard Nixon

92. The Mighty Mo

93. Leviticus 25:10

94. In the first row behind the "whites only" seating

95. Department of Homeland Security

96. Nine

97. World War I, World War II, Korean War, and Vietnam War

98. True. He died before they started producing them.

99. Allman Brothers Band

100. Eight (John Adams, John Quincy Adams, Rutherford Hayes, Theodore Roosevelt, Franklin Roosevelt, John F. Kennedy, George W. Bush, and Barack Obama)

ACTIVITIES
BY SEASON

Just about every experience mentioned in this book can be accomplished at any time of the year. However, there are a few things that are only possible in certain seasons.

Plus, some things are just better to experience at certain times of the year.

Here's a quick guide to some of those seasonal experiences:

SPRING

Go kayaking in the Everglades, 74

Have a picnic at Falls Park in Greenville, SC, 67

Attend the Indy 500, 60

SUMMER

Kansas City Fountains, 102

Eat Thomas Jefferson Ice Cream at Mount Rushmore, 52

Experience the Drive-In, 4

Enjoy a Beer at Frosty Bar on Put-in-Bay, 43

FALL

WINTER

INDEX